MW01200750

Marek J. Murawski

Luftwaffe
versus
USAAF 8th Air Force
vol. I

KAGERO

Contents

Luftwaffe versus USAAF 8th Air Force vol. I • Marek J. Murawski
First edition • LUBLIN 2013

ISBN: 978-83-62878-60-4

© All rights reserved. With the exception of quoting brief passages for the purposes of review, no part
of this publication may be reproduced without prior written permission from the Publisher

Editing: **Marek J. Murawski**
Translation and English version editing: **Kazimierz Zygadło**
Photos: **Author's records, Kagero's records**
Cover illustration: **Arkadiusz Wróbel**
Colour plates: **Janusz Światłoń, Arkadiusz Wróbel**
DTP: **Łukasz Maj, KAGERO STUDIO**

Oficyna Wydawnicza KAGERO
www.kagero.pl • e-mail: kagero@kagero.pl, marketing@kagero.pl

Editorial office, Marketing, Distribution:
KAGERO Publishing Sp. z o.o., ul. Akacjowa 100, os. Borek, Turka,
20-258 Lublin 62, Poland, phone/fax (+48) 81 501 21 05

The Americans enter the European Theatre of Operations

On December 11, 1941, Germany and Italy, fulfilling obligations of the Axis treaty with Japan, declared war on the United States. It turned out to be a fateful decision. The Americans quickly switched to war economy and became the primary supplier of war materiel for the British and Soviets already fighting the Nazi Germany and Italy and also soon joined the fight themselves. During the first half of the year, defeating Germany, although a priority on paper, had to be put on the back burner, as Japan had to be stopped in the Pacific. Only the victory at Midway allowed the Americans to sent their air force to Europe.

The preliminary scope of the American air force participation in the war with Germany was established on January 13, 1942 in Washington. The American air force along with the RAF was to take part in offensive operations against the German home territory. The mutual declaration regulating these matters was signed by President Roosevelt and Prime Minster Churchill. It served as the basis for the plan code named "Rainbow", according to which four heavy bombardment groups and three fighter groups were to be stationed in Great Britain. Later, they were to be reinforced to a total of 21 bomber and 11 fighter groups.

The following plan, code named "Bolero", regulated the entirety of issues related to preparation, redeployment and organization of the American military forces in Great Britain. On February 23,

The deadliest Luftwaffe fighter in the summer of 1942 was Focke-Wulf Fw 190 A-3 powered by 1700 hp BMW 801 D-2 engine which enabled it to reach the maximum speed up to 660 km/h.

Compact form of the Fw 190 A-3 fighter with the camouflage of the wings upper surfaces clearly visible.

1942, Headquarters VIII Bomber Command (VIII BC) of the USAAF 8th Air Force was established under Brig. Gen. Ira C. Eaker. Operational units were Heavy Bombardment Groups (BG) made of four Bombardment Squadrons (BS). In the initial period each squadron consisted of nine aircraft. For combat missions the bombardment group sent three squadrons on a rotation basis. First bomber units equipped with Boeing B-17 Flying Fortress aircraft reached England at the beginning of July 1942.

On May 5, 1942 Maj. Gen. Carl A. Spaatz assumed command of the newly formed USAAF 8th Air Force. The 8th Air Force Staff was relocated to Great Britain on June 18, 1942.

The fundamental objective of the American strategic bombardments was the destruction of the German air force, therefore, the main target were aircraft and aircraft engine factories. Shipyards and submarine naval bases were other priority targets, as their destruction would turn the scales in the battle of Atlantic in favour of the Allies. Following the annihilation of the Luftwaffe's fighter force and Kriegsmarine's submarines the bombing raids were to paralyze communications system and then power plants along with liquid fuel production facilities.

First American air force units became operational on August 15, 1942. These were 97. BG composed of 340., 342. and 414. bombardment squadrons, as well as, 31. FG equipped with British Spitfire VB fighters.

On August 17, 1942, twelve B-17 Flying Fortress of the 340. Bomber Squadron from the 97. Bomber Group, escorted by four RAF squadrons of the 11

Fighter Group, equipped with the most modern fighter of the time – the Spitfire IX, bombed the marshalling yard, engine house and repair workshop at Rouen-Sotteville. The American bomber formation was led by Col. Frank A. Armstrong Jr., Commander of the 97. BG. On board B-17E, 41-9023, leading the second section of six bombers, was the commander of VIII BC, Brig. Gen. Ira C. Eaker. After take off, the American machines formed up two flights made of six planes each. These were made of two V-formations made of three planes each, arranged in such a way, that the leading plane of the second formation was on a line coming through the leading plane and its right side wingman of the

Commander of III./JG 26, Maj. Josef "Pips" Priller in the cockpit of Fw 190 A fighter.

Commander of I./JG 26, Hptm. Johannes Seifert posing in the foreground of his Focke-Wulf Fw 190 A.

Fw 190 A-3 stationed near the English Channel. Due to their low rate of fire of the wing-mounted 20 mm MG FF/M cannons, they were removed in the combat units.

first formation. The Americans dropped 16,700 kg of bombs from 7,000 metres on the largest railway junction in the northern France. However, their aim was poor and only a single bomb scored a direct hit on the engine house destroying four train engines and while some were damaged. Despite the anti-aircraft fire American bombers managed to return to base safely. Fighter escort repulsed the attack of II./JG 26 aircraft loosing three Spitfires of the 401 and 402 Squadrons. Germans reported downing four enemy fighters, one for Lt. Caderbach, Ofw. Philipp, Lt. Sternberg and Uffz. Vogt. American gunners downed Fw 190 A-3, W.Nr. 5332, flown by Lt. Herbert Horn 3./JG 2. German pilot died in the wreckage of his aircraft. The first B-17 gunner of the USAAF 8th Air Force credited with downing Luftwaffe's aircraft was Sgt. Ken Rest, ball turret

gunner of the B-17E "Birmingham Blitzkrieg" of 414. BS.

Conclusions for the future operations were drawn from the results of the first bombardment. Too few planes were sent to destroy such a large target, insufficient training of the crews resulted in poor aim and formation was stretched, which reduced efficiency of defensive fire. Moreover, the escorting Spitfires were four minutes late for the randezvous with the bombers.

This action was the beginning of a series of precision daylight bombardments conducted by large formations of four-engine bombers. It was in accordance with convictions of the high-ranking officers of the U.S. Air Force, who thought that Germany can only be defeated by strategic bombardments.

Pilots of JG 26 during the combat readiness period in the summer of 1943.

On August 19, 1942, the British landed at Dieppe. American bombers supported their allies conducting an air raid at 11.30 against Abbeville airfield with twenty four B-17E bombers. Twenty two Flying Fortress bombers reached the target and their bombs damaged two Fw 190 A fighters stationed there. Luftwaffe, being busy at Dieppe, did not intervene. On the next day, August 20, 1942, eleven B-17s of the 97. BG attacked the Amiens/Longeau marshalling yard. Fighters of III./JG 26 tried to intercept the bombers on their way back, but the escorting Spitfires forced them back with ease.

On August 21, 1942, formation of twelve Flying Fortress bombers was supposed to bomb a shipyard in Rotterdam. It was a very ambitious operation, because due to the fact that the distance between the target and airfields in the south-eastern England was considerable, the bombers would not be escorted by fighters on their entire route. Nine Focke-Wulf Fw 190 A fighters of II./JG 1 attacked the American formation just when it was flying without fighter cover. According to the official war diary of the German fighter unit "The operation was conducted by nine Fw 190, led by Oblt. Olejnik. Formation spotted the enemy in sector 3223 and engaged in sector 3368. These were nine Boeing machines, flying in

tight formation. Repeated attacks were futile. Strong defensive fire of the tail gunners. The only "success" worthy of mention is the fact that all attacked Boeings made an emergency bomb drop over the sea"[1].

One of the bombers, B-17E "Johnny Reb" was damaged. Well-aimed 20 mm round hit the cockpit and killed the co-pilot, 2/Lt. Donald A Walter. Pilot, 2/Lt. Richard F. Starks had his hands burned and handed the controls over to the bombardier, 2/Lt. E. T. Sconiers, who safely piloted the machine back to England. Focke-Wulf 190 A-2, W. Nr. 2116, flown by Ofw. Detlef Lüth, was hit in the radiator by tail gunners and crash-landed at Katwijk, sustaining 10% damage.

Another bombing raid was conducted on August 24, 1942, by twelve B-17E aircraft of 97. BG against the shipyard at Le Trair. On their way back to England the bombers were attacked by a dozen Fw 190 A of II./JG 26. However, their pilots were unable to penetrate the fighter cover and reported shooting down five Spitfires without any loses. The British 402 RAF Squadron lost two planes in this combat, two others were damaged and their pilots were wounded, but they managed to return to England.

On August 27, 1942, nine B-17E headed for Rotterdam. Seven of them reached the target, but this

The B-17 prototype designated Model 299 was first shown on July 17, 1935.

time German fighters did not intervene. On the next day, August 28, fourteen Flying Fortress bombers were to attack the Potez aircraft factory at Meaulte. Only eleven aircraft reached the target, but their bombs caused no serious damage. On their way back, the bomber's formation, escorted by numerous Spitfires, was attacked by Fw 190 A of II./JG 26 and Bf 109 of 11.(Höhen)/JG 2 near Le Havre. German fighters were unable to reach the bombers, but reported shooting down three Spitfires. Pilots of the 611 RAF Squadron shot down on Bf 109 G-1, W. Nr. 14065, "White 5" of 11.(Höhen)/JG 2, flown by Fw. Helmut Baudach, who was wounded.

Bombing raid conducted by thirteen Flying Fortress machines on August 29, 1942, against the JG 26 base at Courtrai-Wevelghem in Belgium was a success. It caused serious damage to ground installations and heavy loses in auxiliary personnel. The quick reaction flight led by Hptm. Priller was caught completely off guard and had not managed to take off before the raid began.

At the beginning of September 1942 the USAAF 8th Air Force was reinforced by bombers of the 301. BG. The new unit had its baptism of fire on September 5, 1942, when twenty-five B-17s of the 97. BG

and twelve of the 301. BG attacked the marshalling yard at Rouen. Only thirty-one bombers reached the target and their aim was rather poor, as only 20% of the bombs hit the target area. The city suffered the most, 140 French were killed and 200 were wounded. Returning bombers were attacked first by the fighters of JG 2, which reported shooting down two Spitfires (Uffz. Gerhard Heinz of 6./JG 2 and Ofw. Josef Heinzeller of 3./JG 2) and then, over the sea, by II./JG 26. The second attack of the German fighters was very successful and ended in downing of six Spitfires. German losses were much lower, British fighters shot down only one Fw 190 A-3, W. Nr. 2237 of 1./JG 2 and its pilot Fw. Alois Immerl was wounded. One Bf 109 G-1, W. Nr. 10312, "White 4" of 11.(Höhen)/JG 2 was also damaged in about 20%.

On the same day, the *Queen Elizabeth* arrived at Greenock carrying the personnel of two new bombardment groups – 93. and 209. BG. She was followed by her sister *Queen Mary*, which brought the personnel of 91., 303. and 305. BG. Four new bombardment groups were to be equipped with B-17 aircraft, while the fifth (93. BG) with B-24 Liberator bombers.

In the late afternoon of September 6, 1942, fifty-one B-17 bombers of the 97. and 301. BG were to attack the Potez aircraft factory at Meaulte. However, only 30 bombers reached the target. Due to the lack of proper coordination , the Spitfire wing that was supposed to cover the Flying Fortresses was late and the bomber's formation was attacked by forty-five Fw 190 A of II./JG 26. German fighters damaged seven bombers and shot down two. First B-17F Flying Fortress, 41-24445, USAAF lost over Europe belonged to the 340. BS, 97. BG and was flown by 2/Lt. Clarence C. Lipsky. It was shot down at 18.55, north-west of Amiens by the commander of II./JG 26, Hptm. Karl-Heinz Meyer. It was his tenth aerial victory. The crew managed to bail out and were taken prisoners. At 10.06, Ofw. Willy Roth of 4./JG 26 scored his seventeenth aerial victory over Le Treport, shooting down the second Flying Fortress. The shot down aircraft was B-17F, 41-9095, "Baby Doll" of the 92. BG, flown by 2/Lt. Leigh E. Steward. The entire crew drowned in the waters of the English Channel.

On the same day thirteen B-17s of the 301. BG attacked airfields in vicinity of St. Omer. The formation, protected by American Spitfires of 133 Squadron, was attacked by fighters of II./JG 2, which managed to shot down two Allied fighters. Aerial victories were reported by Ofw. Paul Marx of the 4./

JG 2 and Uffz. Gerhard Heine of the 6./JG 2. Shortly thereafter, Oblt. Hans Naumann of the 4./JG 26 shot down a Spitfire of 402 RAF Squadron. Germans lost a single Fw 190 A-3, W. Nr. 0526. Its pilot, Lt. Ludwig Spinner died.

Another bombing raid of twenty-nine Flying Fortress bombers took place on September 7, 1942. The target was a shipyard in Rotterdam. Dreadful weather conditions over the North Sea forced majority of the planes to return to England, but nine machines of the 97. and 301. BG had not received the radioed order to abort the operation. Seven headed for Rotterdam and the remaining two for Utrecht. In vicinity of the target American aircraft were attacked by Fw 190 of II./JG 1: "Action of seven Fw 190, led by Oblt. Olejnik (guided by Y-Verfahren system). Formation made contact with the enemy force of 15 Boeings and 25 to 30 Spitfires, Fw. Kaiser was hit in the oil radiator and performed a perfect emergency landing at Katwijk. Lt. Endrizzi (4. Staffeln) did not return from this sortie. He was probably shot down during the first attack. He was last seen disappearing in the clouds in vertical dive. The enemy formation was forced to made an emergency bomb drop. One machine's engine was hit and caught fire, but it burned-out within a short time."[2]

B-17 bombers at the Langley Field in the summer of 1941.

The Boeing factory floor in Seattle full of B-17 fuselages.

German fighters managed to damage B-17F flown by Capt. Aquilla Hughens. Ball turret gunner was killed and three other crew members were wounded. Flying on two engines, with damaged radio and hydraulic system the bomber returned to base. The price for damaging one Flying Fortress and forcing the bombers to made an emergency bomb drop was one Fw 190 A-4, W. Nr. 5566, "White 1". Its pilot, Lt. Karl Endrizzi, was killed. American aerial gunners reported shooting down 12 aircraft, further 10 were probable kills and 12 were reported as damaged. Overstating the number of planes shot down by gunners, was usually due to the fact that one German fighter was fired upon by several gunners and each of them claimed a potential victory.

In September 1942 the number of Luftwaffe fighters stationed in the West reached its peak since the summer of 1940. Stationed in France and Belgium were Stab, I., II. and III./JG.2, as well as Stab. I., II. and III./JG 26, which were subordinate to Luftflotte 3. There were 278 aircraft in total at their disposal. In the Netherlands, Denmark and Northern Germany were Stab. I., II., III. and IV./JG 1, subordinate to Luftwaffenbefehlshaber Mitte.

These had a total of 200 Fw 190 A and Bf 109 G fighters.

Due to the deteriorating weather the next operation of the American four-engine bombers took place on September 26, 1942. Even then, the formation had to turn back shortly after take off because weather conditions made completion of their objective impossible. One of the escort squadrons, American 133 RAF got lost due to its commander's error and after using up their fuel supply, the aircraft either made emergency landings or crashed in vicinity of Brest. Only one pilot managed to return to England, but crashed his machine while landing.

The Command of the 8th AF USAAF planned a large scale operation over France for October 2, 1942. Eighteen aircraft of 97. BG and fifteen of 301. BG were to attack Potez aircraft factory at Meaulte, while six B-17s of 97. BG were assigned to strike against the St. Omer airfield. Apart from RAF fighters, the escort was provided by 23 American Spitfires of 4. FG and 31 P-38 Lightnings of 1. FG for which it was the first combat mission.

First to clash with the Americans were Focke-Wulfs of I./JG 26. The Germans were jumped by Spitfires of the 4. FG and lost two machines, two wounded pilots, Uffz. Günther Rau and Uffz. Hans-Joachim Stoller bailed out. Oblt. Zink, Commander of 2./JG 26 reported shooting down a P-39 Aircobra with white stars. In reality, he only damaged a Spitfire which safely returned to England. At that time pilots of III./JG 26 engaged British Spitfires over the Channel and shot down two planes of 331 RAF Squadron. Both Ogefr. Victor Hager of 7./JG 26 and Lt. Otto Stammberger of 9./JG 26 reported a single aerial victory. They lost only one Fw 190 A of 9./JG 26, its pilot managed to bail out.

Six B-17s reached the Wizernes airfield near St. Omer without any problems and dropped their well aimed bombs. Germans lost some ground crew members, two liaison aircraft were also destroyed. Some fighters of 1./JG 26, which were late to intervene, attacked Lightnings of the 1 FS. Uffz. Stoller of 2./JG 26 shot down one P-38F of 71. FS, its pilot, Lt Young, was pronounced MIA.

At that time the main formation of American bombers was attacked by III./JG 2, II./JG 26 and two high-altitude squadrons equipped with Bf 109 G-1 fighters. After fierce combat with the escort majority of the attacking Luftwaffe fighters managed to force their way to the Flying Fortress bombers. However, the effects of their attack were meagre. None of the bombers were shot down, six were damaged, including one heavily damaged – B-17, 42-24397, "Phyllis" of 301. BG. Three members of its crew were wounded.

During combat with the escort, Germans reported shooting down two Spitfires (Lt. Helmut Hoppe of 6/JG 26 and Ofw. Friedrich Hartmann of 9/JG 2) and one B-17 (Lt. Günther Behrend of 9/JG 2). Escorting Spitfires downed three aircraft of the III./JG 2. Uffz. Rudolf Engstfeld of 7/JG 2 (Fw 190 A-3, W. Nr. 0455) and Uffz. Werner Dollberg of 7/JG 2 (Fw 190 A-3, W. Nr. 0551, "White 1") were killed. The third plane, Fw 190 A-3, W. Nr. 5290 made an emergency landing, being 20% damaged. Its pilot was unscathed. Fw 190 A-2, W. Nr. 25 411, "White 5", flown by Oblt. Elmar Goecke of 4./JG 26 was hit while attacking American bombers from the rear with altitude advantage. German pilot, although seriously wounded, managed to land, but died in hospital on the following day. Fw 190 A-4, W. Nr. 47 057, "Brown 3" of 6./JG 26, damaged by Spitfires, managed to reach Cambrai and while landing crashed into Fw 190 A-4, W. Nr. 5644, standing on manoeuvring area. Both aircraft had to be scraped, and the pilot of the landing Focke-Wulf, Lt. Rudolf Leuschel was wounded. Escorting Spitfires also shot down Messerschmitt Bf 109 G-1, W. Nr. 10 307, "Black 6", but the pilot managed to bail out.

Boeing B-17E bomber, this variant was delivered to England in the summer of 1942 and debuted over the Western European theatre on August 17, 1942. Its maximum payload was 3,628 kg.

Harsh autumn of 1942

On October 2, 1942, 8.AF conducted thirteen bombing raids against targets in the northern France. Bombers flew a total of 317 combat missions with the loss of only two aircraft, which was 0.5% of all machines used.

First summary of the results was most satisfactory for staff officers of the VIII. BC, strong defensive armament of the Flying Fortress bombers composed of 12.7 mm heavy machine guns had so far been successful against attacks of German fighters. It was stated that a tight four-engine bomber formation did not need its own fighter protection when facing single enemy fighters, because its fire power was enough to repulse such attacks.

American optimistic reports did not take into consideration the element of surprise. Initially, German pilots opened fire from too long a distance, as reflexive sights in their machines were set for dogfight with single-engine enemy fighters with wingspan of approximately 10 metres. The optimum moment to squeeze the trigger was when the silhouette of the enemy plane filled the circle of the reflexive sight entirely, which usually happened at a distance between 100 to 160 metres. However, four-engine bomber with wingspan of about 30 metres already filled in the sights at a distance of 300 to 450 metres, which drastically reduced efficiency of the gunfire. Moreover, it turned out that the armament of German fighters was too weak against large, four-engine bombers. Therefore, its strengthening became a fundamental issue, as General der Jagdfieger Adolf Galland compared the 7.92 mm MG 17 machine guns to firecrackers. The 20 mm MG FF/M cannons were also inefficient due to their low rate of fire. The only effective weapon were 20 mm MG 151 cannons. Moreover, new combat tactics were being developed, because so far bombers had been attacked by single fighters from above and behind. It was totally ineffective against the Flying Fortress squadrons, as the bombers tail armament was the strongest. It was time to attack in tight flight or even squadron formations, when

The arrival of the USAAF 8th Air Force to England implied the need for enormous amounts of fuel and consumables which had to be delivered by Atlantic convoys. Some equipment was provided by the RAF. The photo shows Airspeed Oxford communications aircraft.

the firepower of the attacking fighters would be aggregated.

The next bombing raid of 84 B-17 bombers of 92., 97., 301. and 306. BG and also 24 B-24 Liberator bombers of 93. BG, for which it was the first engagement, took place on October 9, 1942. The steel plant and train yard at Camping de Fives in Lille were primary targets. At 09.12 American formation flew over the British coast near Felixtowe and headed for the English Channel. The bombers were escorted by 156 Allied fighters, but it turned out that coordination failed miserably and the bombers reached France without fighter cover. Before that happened two B-17 of 306. BG had to return to their bases due to technical problems.

The anti-aircraft fire in vicinity of the target dispersed the formation and damaged one of the bombers belonging to 306. BG; its No. 2 engine caught fire. Only 69 bombers dropped their bombs on the designated target, but many of them were duds and failed to explode. Inexperienced crews of 93. and 306. BG dropped their loads on the residential areas far from the target, killing many French civilians. At the same time, Hptm. Josef "Pips" Priller,

Commander of III./JG 26, scrambled his fighters. However, he was unable to determine the ceiling of the incoming American bombers correctly, and his pilots managed to attack the enemy only in the third attempt. The air combat began after the bombardment. Lt. Albert W. La Chasse, bombardier of the Flying Fortress "Snoozy II" of the 306. BG remembered it as follows:

"At about 1,000 yards at three o'clock there immediately appeared, in line astern, a gaggle of Me 109s stalking us with four years' war experience. `Ass-end Charlie' was about to become a 'sitting duck' ! The interphone came alive with voices.

`Top turret: Jerries[3] climbing into the sun behind me.'

'Red lights flashing on the instrument panel; four bombs hung!'

I couldn't bring the doors up with the armed bolts still there. One stray armour-piercing bullet in the right place and boom, no anything!

Bandits[4] were everywhere. Where are those God-damn P-38s? Sounds like typing on loose paper indicated enemy shells were ripping into the ship's skin surfaces. "Snoozy II" began to lag behind the rest of

Boeing B-17E aircraft at one of the airfields.

Fw 190 A-3, "Black 10" of 8./JG 2 at the Brest airfield.

Commodore of JG 2, Maj. Walter Oesau and the Commander of 9./JG 2, Oblt. Siegfried Schnell.

the formation. 'Honest John' McKee's ship tried lagging back with us. Good old 'Honest John'. He tried.

Tracers were coming and going in all directions. 'How can I toggle armed bombs in a canted ship?' I thought. They hadn't taught me that in cadet training. I thought, `Salvo! that's it: dump the whole damn load, bombs, shackles and all.' Now we were headed west, towards the white cliffs of Dover. Then suddenly, S/Sgt Bert E Kaylor, the tail gunner, screamed, `Jerries at six o'clock!' I thought, 'Boy that's right up our butts.' Out of the sun the bastards came. I could feel each gunner's position as they fired. Tail, ball and waist gunners each took turns. Again, where are those P-38s? Now only Truman C Wilder, the ball turret gunner, was still fir-

ing. Oh, oh, a belly attack was coming. All at once a German fighter flew right by our nose with a dirty yellow belly and nose with a white prop' spinner and black-painted corkscrew lines like a top. I tried to contact anyone on intercom but there was no sound."[5]

Rounds fired by the German fighter killed both the first and the co-pilot, radio operator and one of the waist gunners. Only La Chasse, Gise (navigator) and Wissenbeck (tail gunner) survived.

The German pilot probably responsible for that aerial victory was Oblt. Otto Stammberger, swarm commander (Schwarmführer) of 9/JG 26:

"On 9 October the Staffel had just landed under my command at Wevelghem, when around 0830

Boeing B-17E
"Peggy-D" of 342.
BS, 97. BG.

hours we were scrambled. We should climb into the direction of St Omer. However, we didn't gather systematically as when we were flying at a height of 3,500 to 4,000 metres, we already spotted a quite large pile of formidable fat bluebottles, which were approaching from the direction of St Omer. They were American bombers of the Boeing B-17 type. They were not flying in a tight formation, as they flew in three rows and all 'vics' obviously flew higgledy-piggledy. Up to a height of 6,000 metres, vics of Viermots were cruising along and above these I saw the vapour trails of fighter aircraft. In the meantime, the bombers had flown just past the west of Lille. Until we arrived at the bombers, the stream had turned tightly to the left and to the south of Lille, and at last I got into a firing position. We

Control panel in the cockpit of Boeing B-17F.

Norden Bombsight M-1

Norden M-1 bomb-sight used on board the American strategic bombers.

The B-17 mechanic also acted as a gunner operating the upper gun turret equipped with twin 12.7 mm machine guns.

During the Flying Fortresses first combat mission on August 17, 1942, the formation was lead by Col. Frank A. Armstrong, Jr., Commader of 97. BG, flying on board the "Butcher Shop".

During the August 17, 1942 mission, Brig. Gen. Ira C. Eaker, Commander of VIII. BC, was flying on board the B-17E, 41-9023 "Yankee Doodle" of 414. BS, leading the second section of six aircraft.

charged into the single vics with our fighters attacking in pairs. We came in from behind, throttled back and fired our guns. The things grew bigger and bigger and all our attacks were commenced and broken off much too early, as we were afraid of flying into the 'barn doors'. I was wondering why I didn't register any hits, until I thought about the size of the lumps: a wing span of forty metres! Therefore, charge in at much closer range and so fast that nothing would happen to us anyway. Then commence firing, starting with the engines in the left wing. At my third pass, both engines were on fire, and I succeeded in hitting the right outer engine as well, which belched forth smoke, and the 'Kahn' plunged down to the left and towards the ground in wide spirals. At a height of some 2,000 metres, four or five men baled out and to the east of Vendeville and the 'Kasten' crashed."[6]

German fighters, taking advantage of the fact that Allied fighters were not present, attacked in single swarms (flights) from behind with altitude advantage and managed to shot down one Liberator and three Flying Fortresses. Hptm. Priller, who shot down a Liberator, opened the list of aerial victories. Next were the pilots of 7./JG 26, led by Hptm. Klaus Mietusch. Commander of 7./JG 26, Hptm. Mietusch, reported shooting down two Flying Fortress bombers, but these were not confirmed (both heavily damaged bombers reached England, but they were irreparable and were both scrapped). Lt. Walter Meyer of 7./JG 26 shot down a bomber of 92. BG. Lt. Otto Stammberger and Oblt. Kurt Ruppert, both of 9./JG 26, shot down one B-17 each. As many as 36 Flying Fortresses and ten Liberators were damaged, including aforementioned two, which were later scrapped.

Germans lost only one Focke-Wulf Fw 190 A-4, W. Nr. 7043, "White 2" of 7./JG 26. Its pilot, Uffz. Viktor Hager was killed. American gunners reported shooting down 56 enemy fighter, 26 as probable kills and further 20 as damaged. As a result, they were credited with 25 kills, 38 probable kills and 44 damaged enemy planes. These numbers, as a con-

B-17E Flying Fortress of 97. BG taxing for the first combat mission over Europe, August 17, 1942

Focke-Wulf Fw 190 A-3 at an airfield in the Northern France, summer 1942.

firmation of a great victory scored by USAAF in the aerial battle over France, were listed in President Roosevelt's radio address.

On October 20, 1942, Brigadier General Asa N. Duncan, Chief of Staff of the 8th Air Force, issued an order in which German U-boat bases were designated as priority targets for the heavy bombers of the USAAF. On the next day, October 21, 1942, an air raid against the U-boat base at Lorient was executed by 66 Flying Fortresses of 97., 301. and 306. BG and 24 Liberators of 93. BG. Dreadful weather conditions forced majority of American aircraft to return to their bases before they were able to reach the target. Only 15 Flying Fortress bombers of 97. BG continued the mission. German pilots of III./JG 2, after ferocious attacks, repeated for several dozen minutes, managed to shoot down three bombers and damage six others. Americans lost the following bombers: "Francis X" flown by Lt. Francis X. Schwarzenbeck of 342. BS, "Johnny Reb" flown by Lt. Milton M. Stenstrom and 41-24344 flown by Capt. John M. Bennet, both of 414. BS. Oblt. Armin Landmann, Oblt. Bruno Stolle and Uffz. Rudolf Eisele of 8./JG 2 were credited with aerial victories. Germans lost a single Fw 190 A-2, W. Nr. 0333, "White 8" of 8./JG 2. Its pilot, Oblt. Otto Lutter managed to bail out, but his parachute did not open.

American gunners reported shooting down 10 fighters, further 4 as probable kills and 3 damaged.

Despite heavy losses, the American command stated that defensive strength of the heavy, four-engine bombers formation is sufficient enough to consider the threat posed by Luftwaffe fighters to be insignificant. Thus, on October 29, 1942 a plan of concentrated bombing strikes against U-boat bases on the Atlantic coast of France and targets beyond the reach of the fighter escort was prepared. At the end of 1942 bombardment of shipyards and plane

factories in Bremen, Vegesack, Wilhelmshaven and Kiel was planned. Commander of the 8th USAAF assumed that the losses may be at maximum 8% of the forces involved.

On November 1, 1942, 91. BG flew its first combat mission, a strike against Brest, which ended without losing a single USAAF machine. It was repeated on November 7, 1942 by sixty-eight B-17 and B-24 bombers. Due to low cloud ceiling only 43 bombers reached the target, but their bombs missed their mark. About 20 Focke-Wulf Fw 190 A of III./JG 2 also appeared there, but despite ferocious attacks, Luftwaffe pilots managed to shot down only one bomber[7]. Oblt. Bruno Stolle of 8./JG 2 was credited with B-24. American gunners shot down two fighters, two 8./JG 26 pilots were killed – Lt. Herbert Hufnagl (Fw 190 A-3, W. Nr. 2178, "Black 11") and Oblt. Armin Landmann (Fw 190 A-3, W. Nr. 7009).

On the next day, November 8, 1942, 24 bombers of 301. and 306. BG escorted by 15 Spitfire squadrons bombarded the train depot at Lille, while 15 Flying Fortress bombers of 91. BG escorted by six Spitfire squadrons headed for the Abbeville/Drucat airfield.

The second formation was attacked by pilots of II./JG 26, who managed to take off before the raid and shot down two Spitfires VB of 421 RAF Squadron (both British pilots, S/Ldr. F. C. Wilis and F/Sgt. C. A. Davis, were killed). These aerial victories were awarded to Lt. Helmut Hoppe and Uffz. Gerhard Vogt, both of 6./JG 26. Other German fighters made almost 200 attacks against five B-17s of 369. BS, but failed to shot down any bombers. Meanwhile, I. and III./JG 26 and III./JG 2 attacked a larger bombers formation in vicinity of Lille. Oblt. Siegfried Schnell and Lt. Günther Behrendt, both of 9./JG 2, Fw. Günther Toll of 7./JG 2, Uffz. Heinz Klems of Stab I./JG 26, Oblt. Josef Haiböck of 1./

Boeing B-17 Flying Fortress "Stric Nine" of 91. BG taking off the Bassingbourn airfield in England.

JG 26 and Oblt. Fülbert Zink of 2./JG 26 reported shooting down six escorting Spitfires. The real British losses were five Spitfires (four Mk.IX and one Mk.V). A moment later Lt. Gerhard Seifert of 9./JG 26 shot down B-17, 41-24472 of 306. BG, which had been previously damaged by anti-aircraft artillery fire. Fw. Martin Reichherzer of 7./JG 2 (Fw 190 A-3, W. Nr. 2429) was mortally wounded in combat with Spitfires and died in hospital on November 28, 1942.

On November 9, 1942, forty-seven B-17 and B-24 bombers attacked the U-Boat base at St. Nazaire. The VIII. BC ordered the low level bomb drop (7,000 to 8,000 feet, that is 2,200 to 2,500 metres). As many as three Flying Fortress bombers of 306. BG were shot down by the anti-aircraft artillery fire. These losses contributed to issuing of an order which prevented the four-engine bombers from low level strikes.

Another strike at St. Nazaire took place on November 17, 1942. Bombers of 93., 303. and 306. BG were attacked over their target by fifteen Fw 190 A of III./JG 2. German fighters heavily damaged one bomber ("Chennault's Pappy" flown by Cpt. Robert C. Williams). It reached England and was forced to land in Exeter, but it had to be scrapped. Germans lost one Fw 190 A-3, W. Nr. 0248 of 8./JG 2, whose pilot managed to bail out. This plane was credited to Sgt. Kenneth Kurtenbach – tail gunner of the B-17, 41-24602, "Yardbird" of the 303. BG.

On the next day, November 18, 1942, American bombers again appeared over St. Nazaire and were once more attacked by Fw 190 of III./JG 2. Uffz. Herbert Gumprecht of 8./JG 2 shot down the Flying Fortress, "Floozy" of 367. BS, which was a part of 306. BG. Heavily damaged plane ditched in the Bay of Biscay. Its pilot, Lt. Ralph J. Gaston and eight crew members were taken prisoners. Another heavily damaged bomber, "Katy Bug" of 328. BS, 93. BG crashed during a forced landing near Alconbury in England and four crew members were killed. The 8./JG 2 lost two planes shot down by B-17 gunners. These were: Fw 190 A-3, W. Nr. 0435, whose pilot, Oblt. Friedrich Kellner was wounded and Fw 190 A-3, W. Nr. 7008, whose pilot Uffz. Paul Willer was killed.

On November 22, 1942, seventy-six four-engine bombers was supposed to attack the U-boat base at Lorient. However, due to terrible weather conditions only 11 B-17 bombers of 303. BG managed to reach the target. Their bombs did not cause any significant damage.

Meanwhile, Oblt. Egon Mayer, Commander of III./JG. 2 developed a new, unconventional method of attack against four-engine bomber box formation. On the basis of previous observations made by Luftwaffe pilots, Mayer concluded that American bombers' defensive armament is the weakest in the nose section, therefore a head-on attack against the Flying Fortress bombers is the most effective. To repel such an attack, the B-17E and F had only two machine guns in the top turret and two more in the ball-shaped positions placed diagonally in the forward canopy. However, these two machine guns could not fire directly ahead, which left a blind spot between them. According to new tactics, fighter formation was to close on the bombers with an altitude advantage and than overtake it. Those manoeuvres were executed out of range of the Flying Fortress bombers' gun fire. When the German fighters were approximately 3 kilometres ahead of the bombers, they turned and attacked head-on. Closing on

Staff of 7./JG 26 preparing Fw 190 A-4 fighters for combat mission.

Fw 190 A-3 of 4./JG 2.

Supermarine Spitfire Mk. V of the American 308. FS.

Fw 190 A of Stab JG 26.

Commander of 309. FS, Maj. Harold Thyng in the cockpit of Spitfire Mk. V "Mary-James". Mary was his wife's name while James was his son's.

the enemy from the least defended side provided German pilots with comparative safety against the bomber gunners' fire. Although the head-on attack did not expose Luftwaffe pilots to concentrated defensive fire, it required considerable skill and experience. The speed of an attacking fighter was no less than 500-550 km/h, while American bombers were flying at 300 km/h, which added to the combined approach speed in excess of 800 km/h. That gave the fighter pilot very little time to aim, fire and break off the attack at a safe distance from the target. If the distance at which the German pilot opened fire was 450 metres and the attack terminated with pulling the stick at 90 metres from the bomber, there

An unfortunate landing of a III./JG 2 pilot. The camouflage of the upper wing surfaces is clearly visible.

Maj. Gerhard Schöpfel, Commander of JG 26 in the cockpit of Fw 190 A-3, W.Nr. 2162 at the St. Omer-Wizernes airfield.

Spitfire Mk. V, EN 799 of 31. FG taxing at the Merston airfield, end of August 1942.

Commander of III./JG 2, Hptm. Egon Mayer at his Fw 190 A-3, W.Nr. 130 435, "White 7".

Contrails marking the patch of Flying Fortress formation.

were no more than 2-3 seconds to fire. Well-trained pilots, able to instantaneously estimate the distance and appropriate deflection, were necessary for performing such accurate attacks. For less experienced fighters sensing the right moment to open fire was very difficult. They broke away the attack too early and did not score any hits or scored too few, which were not enough to shot down a four-engine bomber. Sometimes, they broke away too late and rammed the bomber. Twenty millimetre cannon round hits were necessary to shot down a bomber,

7.92 mm rounds had virtually no effect, unless by pure chance they hit some unarmoured sections of the airframe or crew members. It took about twenty 20 mm round hits to down a four-engine bomber. To score those twenty hits about 1,000 rounds had to be fired, which equalled to a 23-second burst, as the hit rate was no more than 2%. Statistically, ten head-on attacks were required to shot down a single bomber. Naturally, there were cases in which Flying Fortress bombers were shot down even by a single hit, but on the other hand, some planes hit by 30 or more rounds managed to return to base.

New tactics were first employed on November 23, 1942 while repulsing the bombing raid of 58 B-17 bombers against the U-boat base at St. Nazaire. Technical difficulties and poor weather conditions forced 22 bombers to return to England before they reached the target. Near St. Nazaire American formation was attacked head-on by fighters of III./JG 2, led by Oblt. Egon Meyer. The new tactics had a staggering effect on the bomber crews, as John Comer, top turret gunner of B-17 recollects: "Suddenly (copilot Herb) Carqueville screamed over the intercom: `Fighter coming in twelve o'clock level-get him! Get him! Get him!" I was tracking four suspicious fighters at nine o'clock and wheeled around just in time to get

Maj. Walter Oeasu, Commander of JG 2 and Ofw. Josef Wurmheller.

Fw 190 A wrecked while landing at the Beauvais/Nivillers on September 4, 1942.

my sights on the fighter attacking us. It was headed straight for our nose spitting deadly 20 mm cannon shells and 30 calibre machine gun bullets. I was so fascinated by the sight that I froze! Did not fire a shot!! Neither did the Bombardier nor the Navigator - the only other guns that could bear on a frontal attack! Light flashes from the leading edge of the fighter signalled how many cannon shells were being fired at us. I could hear some projectiles striking the airplane. It was a spectacle that drove deep into my memory. The fighter turned his belly to us and slipped into a beautiful barrel roll under our right wing and dived out of range.

Carqueville was boiling mad! He exploded over the intercom: "What th' hell's the matter with you

sunnuvabitches? You're supposed to be gunners! Why didn't you shoot?. . . "

He was furious and he should have been, because there was no excuse for failure to fire. I have relived those traumatic moments many times and I can still feel the mesmerizing power that prevented my hand from pressing that firing switch. Why didn't we fire? I will never know for sure."[8]

During the first attack, at 13.25, Oblt. Egon Meyer shot down one Flying Fortress. After a while Luftwaffe fighters turned round and struck for the second time. Then, at 13.34, Uffz. Friedrich May of 8./JG 2 and again Oblt. Egon Meyer shot down a B-17 each. The third attack gave victory to Oblt. Siegfried Schnell of 9./JG 2, who shot down a B-17 at 13.46.

The fifth, final victory at 14.00 was again reported by Oblt. Egon Mayer. Germans lost one Fw 190 A-4, W. Nr. 7061, "White 10", whose pilot, Uffz. Theodor Angele of 7./JG 2 was killed.

In direct vicinity of St. Nazaire Americans lost four Flying Fortress bombers: two of the 91. BG, flown by Commanders of 322. BS ("Sad Sack" flown by Maj. Victor Zienowicz) and 324. BS (41-24503, "Pandora's Box", flown by Maj. Harold Smelser), as well as 41-24568, "Lady Fairweather" of 359. BS, 303. BG (flown by Capt. Charles G. Miller) and B-17 of 369. BS, 306. BG, flown by 1/Lt. Clay Isbell. The fifth B-17 of 91. BG, "The Shiftless Skonk" crashed at Leavesden, Hertfordshire and five crew were killed.

Upon receiving the report of III./JG 2 action on November 23, 1942, General der Jagdflieger, Obstlt. Adolf Galland submitted a letter to all Luftwaffe fighter wings in which he wrote:

"I herby express my gratitude to Commander of III./JG 2, Oblt. Mayer for his extraordinary action on 23.11.42 which resulted in scoring personal victories over three four-engine bombers.

Bold, individual combat achievement led to and sustained important conclusions. The same attack tactics, employed in repeated examples, confirmed its effectiveness by aerial victories.

Henceforth, the concern of a flying formation's leader will be to take advantage of these confirmed weaknesses by efficient and determined direction of swarms, flights, as well as squadrons and if possible even larger formations during strong and constantly repeated attacks.

Apart from that, the work will continue to strengthen the armament of our fighters and development of even more efficient ammunition will not be stopped. Attached you will find an analysis of the III./JG 2 Commander's report to be forwarded to all pilots."[9]

The next action of the 8. AF strategic bombers took place on December 6, 1942. The target of eighty-five B-17 bombers was the train depot at Lille, while nineteen B-24 attacked the JG 26 base at Abbeviller/Drucat airfield. Both formations were escorted by 16 Spitfire RAF squadrons.

When the group of 19 Liberators designated to create diversion approached the coast of France, British radars detected a large group of Luftwaffe fighters heading towards the bombers. As a result, the B-24 bombers were called back to England, except six aircraft that did not receive the radio signal to abort the mission. They continued flying towards Abbeville. After dropping their bombs the Liberators were attacked by a dozen or so aircraft of

Hptm. Wilhelm Gäth of Stab JG 26.

Fw 190 A-3 of Stab III./JG 26 taxing for take off at the Abbeville-Drucat airfield.

Spitfire Mk. V, QP•V of 2. FS at the Kenley airfield, September 1942.

II./JG 26. However, German attacks were rather feeble and were easily repulsed by the air gunners. Only a few minutes later fighters of I./JG 26 arrived at the scene and launched a more aggressive attack. Uffz. Heinrich Schnell of 3./JG 26, attacking head-on, shot down B-24D, 41-23786 of 68. BS, 44. BG, flown by 1/ Lt. James D. Dubard Jr. In combat with the escorting Spitfires, Oblt. Rolf Hermicher of 3./JG 23 reported shooting down one British fighter. However, I./JG 26 also suffered heavy losses. Ogefr. Erich Eschke (Fw 190 A-4, W. Nr. 0683, "White 6") and Lt. Friedrich Graf Uiberacker (Fw 190 A-4, W. Nr. 5607, "White 5") were killed.

The main B-17 formation reached Lille with significantly reduced number of only 37 bombers. In vicinity of the target pilots of II./JG 26 attacked the escort and reported shooting down three Spitfires (one for Lt. Kurt-Erich Wenzel of 6./JG 26, Uffz. Gerhard Vogl of 6./JG 26 and Uffz. Peter Crump of 5./ JG 26 each). A moment later B-17s were attacked by pilots of II./JG 1, two of whom, Ofw. Hans Ehlers and Uffz. Eugen Wloschinski, both of 6./JG 1, reported shooting down two enemy planes. Americans lost a single machine directly over the target. It was B-17, 41-24553, "Cherry" of 422. BS, 305. BG, flown by Lt. William A. Prentice. Only Lt. Henry

Fw 190 A-4 of 6./JG 2.

A peaceful moment at 8./JG 2 airfield. In the background Fw 190 A-3, W.Nr. 2187, "Black 11" can be seen.

J. Webber and Lt. Harry O. Williams managed to bail out from the burning aircraft. Both airmen were taken prisoners and Williams, severely wounded, died a few days later. Seven Flying Fortress bombers were damaged.

On December 12, 1942, VIII. BC planned bombing raids against Luftwaffe service facility and depots at Romilly-sur-Seine. Since the target was far beyond the reach of the escort fighters, some diversion was also planned to lure the Luftwaffe fighters away. The main formation, composed of Flying Fortress bombers of 303. and 306. BG, was tailed shortly after crossing the French coast by aircraft of 9./JG 26 which had taken off from the Beaumont-le-Roger airfield at 11.51. Germans waited patiently until the escort left the bombers and only then began their attack. Focke-Wulfs attacked the American bombers one after another, as if it was a training exercise. After a shot engagement, at 12.15, B-17, 41-24582, "One O'Clock Jump" of 358. BS, 303. BG flown by Capt. William Frost went into a flat spin and crashed into the ground. Five crew members were taken prisoners, two were killed and three were hidden by the Resistance and later transported back to England. This aerial victory was the first one for Uffz. Erich Schwarz. At 12.35 another Flying Fortress was shot down by Uffz. Walter Lühs. B-17F, 41-24585, "Wulf-Hound" flown by 1/Lt. Paul Flickenger of 360. BS, 303. BG, managed to crash land. The Americans failed to burn their machine and it was captured by

the enemy. Four crew members were taken prisoners and six were rescued by the Resistance.

Experts from the Luftwaffe's experimental facility in Rechlin quickly put the aircraft back into flyable condition and she became the first B-17 used by the German Air Force. In combat with the returning escort fighters pilots of I. and II./JG 26 reported shooting down five Spitfires without loosing a single aircraft. British documents confirm the loss of two Spitfires Mk.VB and two Mk.IX machines.

On December 20, 1942, VIII BC conducted another operation against the Luftwaffe service facility at Romilly-sur-Seine. One hundred and one bombers including eighty B-17s of 91., 303., 305. and 306. BG, as well as twenty-one B-24s of 44. BG escorted by 12 British and American Spitfire squadrons took part in that engagement. Earlier, the Fighter Command conducted four smaller operations in the Pas de Calais area to lure out the Luftwaffe fighters. However, these actions took place to late and their result was opposite to what was expected. Their aim was to make Germans take off earlier, fly aimlessly for several dozen minutes and return to base to refuel. In the meantime the bomber formation would arrive and safely reach the target, since most Luftwaffe fighters would be busy refuelling. However, American bombers arrived much earlier and although some German fighters returned to their bases, majority of II. and III./JG 26 machines headed for Dieppe to intercept the coming bombers. Luftwaffe fighters tailed American formation waiting for the escorting Spitfires to return to England. At 11.55 they began head-on attack. Their target were B-17s of 91. BG. First to score a victory was the commander of III./JG 26, Hptm. Josef Priller, who at 12.02 shot down B-17F, 41-24452 (flown by Lt. Robert S. English). The second was the commander of II./JG 26, Hptm. Karl-Heinz Meyer, who at 12.11 shot down the Flying Fortress nicknamed "Danellen", flown by Lt. Dan W. Carson. Luftwaffe fighters kept repeating their attacks for the next hour. Two more Flying Fortresses were heavily damaged. These were: "Chief Sly" of 332., flown by 1/Lt. Bruce Barton, which managed to return to England but was wrecked after crash landing near Fletching, Sussex and "Rose O'Day" (flown by Capt. Ken Wallick) which managed to return safely to base at Bassingbourn.

When the fighters of II. and III./JG 26 had to return to base to be refuelled and rearmed, American formation was attacked by III./JG 2 accompanied by machines from the 9./JG 26. Their target were B-17 bombers of 367. BS, 306. BG. Uffz. Alfred Niese of 9./JG 26 was the first to attack and at 12.55 he shot down B-17F, 42-5071 (flown by Lt. Danton J. Nygaard). German rounds hit the nose, cockpit and then the fuselage of the bomber. It went into a flat spin and left the formation. Pilot, wounded in the hand and with burned face along with the bombardier managed to bail out through the smashed nose. The only other crew member who survived was Lt. Frank Leasman. The second Flying Fortress was shot down at. 13.10 by Lt. Otto Stammberger of 9./JG 26: "The second Viermot I brought down was over Paris on 20 December 1942. I managed to shoot down a Boeing in a head-on attack, the machine turning over on its back and diving down with a jerk, and me being able to just pull up and over it. I felt certain that I must have hit the pilots; a burst of the four 2 cm cannons and the two machine guns from our Focke-Wulf into the cockpit (which was only built with sheets of glass or plastic), was guaranteed to be deadly, if we managed to score a hit!"[10]

On their way back to England the Flying Fortress bombers were once more attacked over the French coast of the English Channel by a few fighters of 4./JG 26. The scored the "Staffelabschuß" (aerial victory for the squadron) by finishing off one B-17 of 303. BG.

Fw-190 A-3, W. Nr. 0544 flown by Lt. Fritz Probst of 7./JG 2 ran out of fuel and the pilot had to bail out, but he hit a tree and died on the spot. Some

Hptm. Josef Priller, Commander of III./JG 26 sharing his impressions with fellow pilots.

P-38F Lightning, s/n 41-7652 of 14. FG after a flight from Iceland to Scotland.

other fighters of JG 26 also ran out of fuel and were forced to crash land. At least two were destroyed and the remaining ones were damaged.

The final operation of the VIII. BC in 1942 took place on December 20. Seventy-seven B-17 bombers attacked the U-boat base at Lorient. For the first time American used a new formation named "combat box". It was invented by commander of 303. BG, Col. Curtis LeMay. Three squadrons, minimum six planes each, flew in vertical wedge-shape formation. Each squadron was at a different altitude and the aircraft of the central squadron were in the forward position. Six aircraft of each squadron flew in two three-aircraft flights. In case the squadron dispatched more than six planes, V-formations of four machines flying in diamond-shape formation were used. A bombardment group "Combat box" formation made of three squadrons was 350 metres wide, 300 metres high and 300 metres long. Three bombardment groups flying together took positions next to each other, creating a bomb wing formation. Such formation of 60 planes was 950 metres wide, 800 metres high and 400 metres long. In such formation individual bombers, V-formations, squadrons and groups had mutual support of the air gunners, which allowed for concentration of fire from multiple machine guns on a single target.

Over the target American formation was attacked by III./JG 2. Although the Germans reported shooting down as many as eight Flying Fortress bombers, Americans lost only three machines. Aerial victories

Sgt. Ernest Kish, tail gunner of B-24 Liberator "Teggie Ann".

were scored by Oblt. Egon Mayer, Fw. Kurt Knappe, Oblt. Siegfried Schnell, Lt. Georg-Peter Eder, Lt. Brunno Eder, Fw. Walter Eber, Uffz. Friedrich May and Lt. Wilhelm Godt.

By the end of 1942, VIII. BC carried out 26 operations in which four-engine bombers flew 747 combat missions. Thirty-one aircraft were lost, which constituted 4.2% of total strength[11].

American bombers over the Reich – winter 1943

First combat mission of VIII. BC in the New Year 1943 was a bombing raid of eighty-five B-17 and thirteen B-24 aircraft against the U--boat base at St. Nazaire. Only 60 Flying Fortress and 8 Liberator bombers reached the target. On that day a new bombardment scheme was used for the first time. Since the "combat box" formation did not allow for individual bombers' manoeuvres, the bomb drop had to be simultaneous. The right moment was determined by the bombardier of the leading bomber. As there was no radio signal sent from the leading machine, bombardiers in the following aircraft had to watch it closely, to drop their loads at the right time. The fact that bombs of the leading plane had smoke release signals was helpful as the smoke tails were clearly visible even from a distance. The new method guaranteed high concentration of bomb hits on the target provided that the leading plane's bombardier released his bombs right on the target. If his bombs missed, so did the ones dropped by other planes.

German anti-aircraft defence was alert as the radars had already detected American formation at 10.35. At 11.00 fog generators at St. Nazaire harbour were turned on to make it difficult for enemy bombardiers to locate the target. Also, twenty Fw 190 fighters of III./JG 2 stationed at Vannes were scrambled between 11.09 and 11.16. Half an hour later, at 11.46, ten Fw 190 of 8./JG 2 took off from Brest. Fighters of III./JG 2 attacked the formation approaching St. Nazaire from south-east when it was still over the sea. As reported by Luftwaffe pilots, Americans approached in five waves. First three were forced to make an emergency drop and their bombs fell near the mouth of the Loire River. The rest managed to drop 30 well-aimed bombs on

Fw 190 A-4, W.Nr. 5613, B-+- of Stab JG 26.

Briefing of 8./JG 2 pilots at the Brest/Guipavas airfield, October 1942.

the shipyard facilities and the pier. Barrack ship *St. Christian* and an auxiliary minesweeper were sunk. The shipyard was also heavily damaged.

During the air combat that lasted almost 30 minutes, pilots of III./JG 2 reported shooting down as many as 15 B-17 bombers. Oblt. Egon Mayer (including one HSS[12]) and Oblt. Siegfried Schnell scored two aerial victories each. Lt. Ottfried Philipp, Uffz. Wolfgang Galiga, Lt. Georg-Peter Eder, Oblt. Erich Hohagen, Lt. Franz Rösle, Lt. Benno Eder, Ofw. Friedrich Hartmann, Oblt. Ferdinand Müller, Lt. Friedrich Potzler, Fw. Karl-Heinz Munsche, Lt. Friedrich Fleischmann and Uffz. Friedrich May were all credited with one bomber. Actual American losses were 7 shot down B-17s and 3 B-24s which crashed on their return to England. Forty-four B-17s and three B-24s were damaged. Human casualties included 5 killed, 70 MIA and 29 wounded. The III./JG 2 lost three aircraft, two due to engine failures (Fw 190 A-4, W. Nr. 7074, "White 2" of 7./JG 2 and Fw 190 A-4, W. Nr. 7068, "Yellow 3" of 9./JG 2, its pilot, Lt. Karl Höfer, died). Fw 190 A-4, W. Nr. 7064 of 8./JG 2 was shot down by the USAAF bombers. American air gunners reported shooting down 14 enemy planes, 18 as probable kills and 4 as damaged.

Another aerial battle with four-engine USAAF bombers took place on January 13, 1943. Shortly after 14.00, 72 Flying Fortress bombers attacked the area of Lille, Finally, 159,800 kg of bombs were dropped by 64 aircraft on designated targets. Twenty-four bombers attacked "Ateliers d'Hellemmes" train factory, while 40 remaining ones dropped their bombs on the steel plant and the power station. Fw 190 of I. and III./JG 26 took off to intercept the American formation. German fighters had time to form for a head-on attack, and they made contact with the bombers of 305. BG before they reached Lille. Luftwaffe pilots damaged 10 enemy planes and shot down one B-17 bomber flown by Lt. Conrad J. Hilbinger. Commander of 364. BS, Maj. Tom H. Taylor was killed on board B-17 "Dry Martin II". A moment later the Americans lost two more B-17 bombers. Although the Germans reported shooting down three Flying Fortress bombers, only two victories were confirmed. Both Uffz. Erich Scheyda of 3./JG 26 and Ofw. Heinz Kemethmüller of 7./JG 26 were credited with one bomber. Germans suffered no losses, yet American air gunners claimed shooting down 29 Fw 190 fighters, they were finally credited with 6.

Between January 14 and January 24, 1943, a conference took place in Casablanca, where President Roosevelt and Prime Minister Churchill discussed, among other things, the issues concerning the strategic use of air forces. It had a great impact on designation of targets in the Reich and in the occupied territories. The common strategic objective of the Anglo-American air force was: "Progressive destruction and dislocation of the German military, industrial, and economic system, and the undermining of the morale of the German people to a point where their capacity for armed resistance is fatally weakened."[13]

The following hierarchy of objectives was established:

1. German submarine construction yards and U-boat bases,

2. German aircraft industry and Luftwaffe facilities, especially those connected with fighter aircraft,

3. Transportation and communication routes,

4. Oil and other fuel plants,

5. Ball bearing plants, war industry and other targets.[14]

Results of aerial battles that took place within the last few months and experience acquired made it clear to the German Air Force Command that combat units should be equipped with new types of fighter aircraft, better armed and armoured, as soon as possible. Design work on 30 mm MK 103 and MK 108 cannons was accelerated and they went into serial production in the second half of 1943. New types of ammunition were designed for the 20 mm MG 151 cannons that had already been in use.

Here is how Oblt. Karl Borris, commander of 8./JG 26, remembered his combat with four-engine bombers: "These big boxes were a completely unusual target for us. Our sights were set at targeting aircraft of 10-metre wingspan from 100 metres.

The bombers, with their huge wingspan, appeared huge looking through illuminated reticles of our Revis. Despite the fact that the filled in the entire reticle, it turned out that they were out of effective range of our gunfire. Simultaneously, tracers fired by Flying Fortresses' air gunners were buzzing like a swarm of bees around our cockpits. We attacked from behind, with altitude advantage, from below, from above, the side and head-on, all guns blazing. However, with contemporary ammunition it was difficult to score a decisive hit. We perforated the fuselage, sometimes entire metal sheets were flying off, but the only chance for success was a hit in the engine.

Oblt. Ruppert (21 victories) kept on firing at one Boeing on its entire route from St. Omer to Calais. He was hitting it fair and square. The effect: right outboard engine stopped working, right inboard engine was hit so well that it was torn off the airframe and fell to the ground, the left engine was smoking.

A photo taken from a Flying Fortress bomber during the bombing raid against the U-Boat base at Lorient on October 21, 1942. Reinforced concrete submarine pens are indicated by arrows marked "Target".

1/Lt. Riordan in the cockpit of his B-17 of 306. BG.

The crew ceased fire, but the machine continued flying on one engine. To reduce weight American flyers jettisoned flexible machine guns, rest of the ammunition and even bailed out their dead comrades. The Fortress managed to cross the Channel and crash land on the beach in Ramsgate.

In spring of 1943 we finally received the so-called Hexogen-Munition (high explosive ammunition). These were incendiary rounds, which spurted a stream of burning gases on impact. Success was guaranteed. A hit on a large fuel tank caused fire and the plane usually plummeted to ground.

The hit on a bomber usually manifested itself in three ways. If you hit the cockpit, the dead pilot would pull-off or go into a sharp turn, often causing a mid-air collision with a nearby aircraft. A hit in the fuel tank appeared as brightly red flame. The bomber was burning like a torch, left the formation and its crew bailed out through all possible hatches. Moments later it was blown into smithereens. In other

Fw 190 A-4 of Stab JG 26 at the St. Omer-Wizernes airfield.

Focke-Wulf Fw 190 A-3 of IV./JG 1.

Lt. Julius Meimberg of 11./JG 2 during the combat readiness period.

cases the bomber was only damaged. It was marked by a long smoke trail. Too keep up the cruising speed the bomber had to gradually lose its altitude, which separated it from the others. If the escort fighters allowed that, it would be finished off."[15]

On January 23, 1943, seventy-three B-17 bombers headed for the U-boat base at Lorient. At 13.26 thirty-four bombers dropped 86,000 kg of bombs on the harbour, but the damage on the ground was insignificant. When the bombing raid was in progress,

Fw 190 A-3 of I./JG 2 at the Marseilles-Merignane airfield with a Dornier Do 217 E bomber standing next to it.

Refuelling of Fw 190 A-4, "Black 12", flown by the Commander of 8./JG 2, Oblt. Bruno Stolle.

28 Fw 190 of III./JG 2 and 9./JG 26 took off from the airfield at Vannes. American formation, returning to England, was first attacked by 7./JG 2. Its pilots reported shooting down four B-17s (Oblt. Erich Hohagen, Lt. Georg-Peter Eder, Lt. Hugo Dahmer and Fw. Kurt Knappe). Fighters of 9./JG 26 arrived a few minutes later and both Lt. Melchior Kestel and Uffz. Edgar Dörre reported shooting down one B-17 each. The Americans lost five B-17s, all from 303. BG. Two more, one from the 91. BG and one from 303. BG were wrecked during emergency landings in England. The Germans suffered no losses, although Americans claimed shooting down 7 enemy fighters, 7 as probable kills and further five as damaged.

On January 27, 1943, American Air Force opened a new chapter in the history of World War II by bombarding the Reich territory for the first time. The shipyard at Vegesack, which had been build-ing submarines, was the main objective of 91 four-engine bombers (64 B-17s and 27 B-24s), while shipyards and naval base at Wilhelmshaven were secondary objectives. Heavy overcast made it dif-ficult for the Americans to find the target. Formation of B-24 Liberator bombers of 44. and 93. BG mistook Lemmer in the Netherlands for Wilhelmshaven and 23 bombers dropped their load there, but no signifi-cant damage was done. Between 11.10 and 11.13, fifty-three B-17s of the second formation dropped 132,500 kg of bombs on Wilhelmshaven, but most of them fell into the Jade River. At 11.35, two lost Flying Fortresses dropped 5000 kg of bombs on the Emden shipyard.

Fighters of I., II. and IV./JG 1 under command of Maj. Dr. Erich Mix, took off and headed against the coming bombers. Fighters of 1./JG 1, which took off at 10.45 from Javer airfield, were the first to reach Wilhelmshaven. Messerschmitts Bf 109 G-1 with

Boeing B-17F-27-BO, 41-24585, PU•B of 303. BG was the first Flying Fortress to fall into the hands of the Luftwaffe. The photo shows her already in German colours with fuselage markings DL+XC.

Deelen airfield, the base of IV./JG 1. On the right Fw 190 A-3, W.Nr. 437, "White 12" of 10. Staffel is visible.

their weak armament made of 20 mm MG 151 cannon and two 7.92 mm machine guns were not as suitable for destroying Flying Fortress bombers as better-armed Fw 190 A fighters. Fortunately for the Germans, some of these fighters were fitted with two MG 151 cannons mounted in underwing pods (Bf 109 G01/R2 version). Therefore, Messerschmitt pilots reported shooting down four B-17s (Oblt. Frey, Fw. Zick, Lt. Artl, Uffz. Werner), but it cost them five machines and three pilots killed - Uffz. Rolf Bölter (Bf 109 G-1/R2 Y, W. Nr. 14 146, "White 1"), Ofw. Gerhard Witt (Bf 109 G-1/R2 Y, W. Nr. 14 112, "White 4") and Fw. Helmut Speckhardt (Bf 109 G-1/R2 Y, W. Nr. 14 085). Uffz. Müller of 2./JG 1 was lucky, as he managed to bail out. However, his machine, Bf 109 G-1/R2 Y, W. Nr. 14 074 was completely destroyed.

Liberators, which had already reached the Netherlands coast, were attacked by fighters of 4./JG 1,

who claimed two aerial victories (Ofw. Winkler and Fw. Haninger). Air gunners shot down Fw 190 A-4, W. Nr. 0629, "White 10" and its pilot, Uffz. Erhard Bruhnke was wounded and bailed out. Shortly after 12.00 the B-24 formation was also attacked by machines of 12./JG 1. Its pilots reported shooting down two Liberators (Uffz. Löhr and Uffz. Haenel). Air gunners shot down Fw 190 A-4, W. Nr. 5604, "Yellow 3" and its pilot, Fw. Fritz Koch was killed.

This engagement was described by Howard Adams, crew member on board of one of the Liberators, in his diary: "I noticed that two of our ships were missing. Later I found out that they were my friend and West point classmate, 1/Lt. Maxwell W. Sullivan, flying the "Spirit of 76" and a Lt. Nolan B. Cargile, both of the 68th. On talking with the others, I learned what had happened. As they neared the German [border] around 30 enemy fighters came up to meet them - mostly FW 190s and ME 109s. For around a half hour they were under attack and not being able to find their target, they dropped their bombs on a coastal town. During one of the numerous frontal attacks, the Huns scored a hit on "Sully's" No. 3 engine, setting it on fire, which soon grew in fury as he dropped out of formation. Soon the fire had burnt a large section of the wing away and in no time the right wing folded back along the fuselage and "Sully" plummeted down for his last landing. The crews in the other planes watched helplessly as his plane disintegrated in the air and fell into the sea like a burning rag. Two men were seen to jump out and float down towards the sea in their parachutes. A third man jumped, but his chute trailed out behind him never seeming to open fully. Their fate is still unknown[16].

A little while later, another FW 190 came in on a head-on attack aiming at Cargiles's plane. Either through accident or design, as he went to turn away, his wing clipped the wing and then the right tail fin of Cargile's B-24 knocking both off. The FW 190 (flown by Fw. Fritz Koch of 12./JG 1, who died in this attack – Author's note) seemed to fold up and then go into its last dive. With part of his wing gone, the big B-24 dropped away like a fluttering leaf,

finally going into a tight spin - its fate sealed. None of the crew were seen to jump."

Germans reported shooting down a total of eight four-engine bombers. Americans lost two B-24s and one B-17. Luftwaffe losses amounted to four Bf 109 G and one Fw 190. However, American air gunners claimed shooting down 22 fighters, 14 as probable kills and further 13 as damaged.

On February 4, 1943, the second bombing raid of American strategic bombers against a target on German territory was conducted. Thirty-nine B-17s of the 1. BW dropped 92 tons of bombs on industrial district in Emden, but the damage was minimal. On that day IV./NJG 1 stationed in the Netherlands under command of Hptm. Hans-Joachim Jabs took part in the day action against American four-engine bombers for the first time. Bf 110 night fighter pilots reported shooting down three B-17s. One aerial victory was reported by Hptm. Jabs, who had been one of the best destroyer units' pilot (19 day combat victories and further 6 night combat victories against RAF bombers, awarded Knight's Cross on October 1, 1940). The other two Flying Fortress bombers were shot down by Ofw. Grimm and Uffz. Neumann. Among the lost bombers was B-17, "El Lobo" of 305. BG, flown by Lt. Cornelius A. Jenkins. Five

Fw 190 A-3 of IV./JG 1. The bottom part of the engine cowling painted yellow can be seen.

Boeing B-17F armed with two additional 12.7 mm nose-mounted machine guns.

Gen. Curtis E. LeMay, inventor of the "Combat Box" formation, which turned out to be the key to success of the American four-engine bombers in combat with the Luftwaffe fighters.

crew members died in the wreckage. German losses amounted to seven heavily damaged planes and one completely wrecked during crash landing. Despite shooting down three Flying Fortress bombers, success scored by the night fighters was questionable.

Well-aimed defensive fire of American air gunners destroyed one plane and grounded the remaining seven for several days to come, which reduced combat readiness of the night fighter unit.

At 11.27, a lone Flying Fortress was shot down by Hptm. Wickop of 4./JG 1. Shortly before 12.00 bombers flying west of Leer were attacked by Messerschimtt Bf 109 G fighters of 3./JG 1. Uffz. Werner reported shooting down one B-17 and the Germans lost one Bf 109 G-1, W. Nr. 14 108, but its pilot came out unscathed. At 12.31, B-17 formation was attacked by 5./JG 1 which had taken off from the Schipol airfield. Fighters of 4. and IV./JG 1 arrived shortly thereafter. Germans reported shooting down four B-17s, one aerial victory for Uffz. Emerich of 12./JG 1, Ofw. Lüth of 4./JG 1, as well as Uffz. Stellfeld and Uffz. Schmid, both of 5./JG 1. JG 1 lost two pilots: Oblt. Walter Leonhardt (Fw 190 A-4 W. Nr. 5333, "Yellow 6"), commander of 6./JG 1 was shot down over the sea, west of Texel. He managed to bail out, but the search parties failed to find him. Uffz. Rudolf Mayer of the 12. Staffel (Fw 190 A-4, W. Nr. 0564, "Yellow 8") died in the wreckage of his machine, which crashed near Filsum. Additionally, 10./JG 1 lost one more pilot, Uffz. Werner Hitzke, who lost consciousness over Achmer due to altitude sickness and died in a crash of his Fw 190 A-4, W. Nr. 0567, "White 4". Among the shot down USAAF bombers was the second machine of 305. BG, "What's Cookin' Doc?", flown by Lt. William K. Davidson. The entire crew perished. Two planes were also lost by 91. BG and one by 303. BG.

Boeing B-17F "Werewolf" taking of from a makeshift runway at the Dawlish airfield.

Fw 190 A-4 of 6./JG 1 at the Woensdrecht airfield.

The Germans reported a total of nine B-17s shot down, their losses were 3 pilots killed and 4 planes destroyed. Officially, the Americans lost five B-17s. Air gunners claimed shooting down 25 fighters, 8 as probable kills and 6 damaged.

In the early afternoon of February 13, 1943, twenty-three Liberators of the 44. and 93. BG, escorted by four Spitfire squadrons, attacked the harbour at Dunkirk. Twenty-one B-24s reached the target and at 15.39 dropped 62,000 kg of bombs, which caused no significant damage. Despite the fact that they

were late to receive the information about the raid, Fw 190 fighters of II. and III./JG 26, as well as those of 7./JG 2, took off to attack the bombers. Machines of III./JG 26 were the first to made contact with the enemy. They lost two pilots in dogfight with Spitfires of the escort. These were: Uffz. Karl Bruhn (Fw 190 A-4, W. Nr. 5728, "White 6") and Uffz. Johannes Kemper (Fw 190 A-4, W. Nr. 2434, "White 8"), both of III./JG 26. A moment later, pilots of the II./JG 26 and 7./JG 2 joined the fight. One Spitfire was shot down by Commander of II./JG 26, Hptm. Wilhelm-

B-17F "Eight Ball", flown by 1/Lt. Harold Stouse, upon return from the combat mission over Germany, January 27, 1943.

Messerschmitt Bf 109 G-1/R2, W.Nr. 14 095, "Red E" of III./JG 54 wrecked during take off from the Merville airfield, February 13, 1943.

Ferdinand Galland, while Oblt. Erich Hohagen of 7./JG 2 scored one B-24 kill.

Americans lost three B-24s: "Betty Anne/Gallopin Ghost" of 67. BS, flown by Capt. Art T. Cullen was shot down by the anti-aircraft artillery; only pilot and three gunners survived, "Railway Express", flown by 1/Lt. Rufus A. Oliphant Jr. was shot down by Oblt. Hohagen and the entire crew perished, "Captain And His Kids", flown by Capt. Tom Cramer, was wrecked during crash landing on the beach near Sandwich and three crew members died. RAF fighter pilots claimed shooting down 7 Luftwaffe planes, one as probable kill and 3 damaged. Air gunners added another 3 as confirmed kills and one as probable.

On February 16, 1943, seventy-seven B-17s and eighteen B-24s attacked the U-boat base at St. Nazaire. Even before it reached France, 44. BG lost two Liberators in mid-air collision. Between 10.40

and 11.11, sixty-nine four-engine bombers dropped 160,000 kg of bombs on St. Nazaire. Civilian buildings were heavily damaged, but the harbour area suffered almost no damage. When the American bombers turned back and headed for England, at 11.15, they were attacked by I./JG 2 north of Vannes. German fighters, which were soon joined by those of III./JG 2 and 9./JG 26, attacked in waves for the next 45 minutes. Pilots of I./JG 2 reported shooting down four B-17s. Two aerial victories were scored by Lt. Josef Wurmheller of 1./JG 2, while Hptm. Helmut Bolz, Commander of the I./JG 2 and Lt. Horst Hannig of 2./JG scored one bomber each. Lt. Fritz Edelmann of 3./JG 2 scored one B-17 as HSS. Pilots of 9./JG 26 reported shooting down 3 enemy planes, two of those were confirmed. Fw. Edgar Dörre shot down B-17, 42-5175 of the 367. BS, 306. BG, flown by Lt. Joseph A. Downing and

Fw 190 A-5, W.Nr. 5862 of 8./JG 2 at the Brest airfield.

Ofw. Willi Gams of 8./JG 2 posing in front of his Fw 190 A-5, "Black 1" at the Wevelghem airfield.

Uffz. Erich Schwarz downed B-17, 42-5717 of 423. BS, 306. BG, flown by Lt. William H. Warner. German losses were limited to one Fw 190 A-4, W. Nr. 0797 of III./JG 2, damaged by defensive machine gun fire, which had to crash land.

Uffz. Erich Schwarz recollected that action: "We scrambled from Vannes and reached the bombers in time to form up for a frontal attack. They were proceeding toward their target, and could not make even slight course changes without endangering their attack on the U-boat bunkers. They had to fly straight ahead. I chose as my target the highest-flying B-17 on the far right. They had recognized us, as the formation had pulled closer together to strengthen their defences. As I approached to about 1,000 meters, the pilot lost his nerve and pulled up into a steep climb, undoubtedly with the help of his copilot. This exposed the entire belly of his airplane. I followed this movement, and since a fighter is more manoeuvrable than a cumbersome B-17, my six weapons could

B-17F "Southern Comfort" of 305. BG managed to limp back to base on one engine from her bombing raid against Bremmen on February 26, 1943, despite attacks of several Bf 109 G fighters belonging to JG 1.

scarcely miss. Although it was only a short volley, the B-17 could no longer hold its place in formation. I was impressed that a bomber had been capable of such a defensive manoeuvre at 7,000 meters."[17]

American losses amounted to a total of 8 four-engine bombers destroyed, 30 damaged. One crew member was killed, 8 wounded and 81 MIA. Air gunners claimed shooting down 20 Luftwaffe fighters, 12 as probable kills and 2 damaged.

Due to unfavourable weather conditions the third bombing raid of USAAF four-engine bombers against targets in Germany did not take place until February 26, 1943. The objective of 93 bombers, seventy-six B-17s and seventeen B-24s, was thr Focke-Wulf factory in Bremen. However, the city was enveloped in heavy clouds, therefore a secondary objective, submarine base at Wilhelmshaven, was selected. Only 65 bombers reached the target area and dropped 161,000 kg of bombs. The Luftwaffe's NJG 1 night fighters also engaged the bombers. Hptm. Ludwig Becker, one of the night fighter aces with 44 aerial victories, was killed in that action. Pilots of NJG 1 reported shooting down two B-24 bombers (Oblt. Rudolf Sigmund of 10./NJG 1 and Uffz. Georg Kraft of 12./NJG 1).

Pilots of IV./JG 1 had already received signal to scramble at 10.01 and headed for the coming bombers. Among the pilots was Lt. Eberhard Burath: "On February 26th I had my first contact with the four-engined bombers, very personal and exclusive, so to speak. In the usual — and often futile — search for the enemy group after some time as the right outside flyer in a left curve I lost sight of my group and flew alone straight out towards the North Sea. I noticed too late and started looking for my counterparts. In the distance I spotted them and pursued them at full speed. Suddenly they became larger, much too large for fighter planes. Huh? There were the bombers, 60 to 70 of them in a thick formation.

Now what? Fear comes first out of experience and I had none yet. Without thinking I curved toward the bombers and attacked from in front. Shooting out of all tubes I rushed through the formation. Banking, pulling parallel to the front. There a shell nearly caught me, on a perfect trajectory sailing towards me from the left like a red tomato. Nice that those fellows still used tracers so that I could just pull away below. I roared once more through the group, and then it was time to head for the coast, which was still 100 kilometres away. What could the Americans have thought about this 'huge attack of German fighters'? As an 'alibi' at least they left me a clean hit in the engine, but the BMW 801 still ran well on 13 cylinders."[18]

Soon, the remaining fighters of IV./JG 1 arrived at the scene. Ofw. Otto Bach of 12./JG 1 shot down B-17 "Lucy Belle" of 303. BG, flown by 1/Lt. Lloyd Driffin. At. 11.12, twelve Messerschmitt Bf 109 G fighters of 1./JG 1 took off from the Jever airfield. Lt. Heinz Knoke of 2./JG 1 took part in that action:

"Involuntarily I have gone up to full throttle. Attack! I can distinctly see the individual planes. They are for the most part Liberators. They appear plump with pregnant bellies full of bombs. I select a target. I will attack from the front. Clearly the American sits in my sights. Quickly he becomes larger. I feel the buttons on the control stick. Tracer bullets fly over my cabin. They're shooting at me!

At the same time I open fire, pressing both buttons. The recoil of my cannons and heavy machine guns leave my bird shaking lightly. My aim is not good. I can see only a few hits on the right wing. I swoop under the fat stomach of my opponent. The draft of his four propellers shakes me around in such a way that I think for a second that my tail assembly is torn. The combined speeds of our two approaching planes is over 1,000 kilometres per hour. Steeply I pull above to the left. Tracer bullets

A single bar marking first aerial victory scored on February 26, 1943, by Uffz. Heinz Hanke of JG 1 while flying Fw 190 A, W.Nr. 5701.

Lt. Heinz Knoke and Oblt. Hugo Frey, Commander of 2./JG 1, at the Jever airfield, end of February 1943. In the background Bf 109 G-1 Y, W.Nr. 14 049, "Black 3" can be seen.

from the guns of the Liberator follow me. Damned iron-filled air! 300 four-engine bombers carry 4,800 heavy machine guns. If only a third of those are firing, that still means a hail of fire for us.

For the second time I attack, this time from the front and below, and shoot until I am within ramming distance. My shots hit! I let myself fall away below. In falling away I turn my head. My Liberator is burning underneath. It turns in a wide curve to the right away from her group. We are about 8,000 meters high. From behind and above, once again I attack. Strong defensive fire comes toward me.

My high explosive shells hit in the top side of the fuselage and the right wing. With both hands I clasp the control stick. The fire has overcome the right side

of the wing. The inside engine has stopped. The wing has ripped away! Perpendicularly the huge fuselage falls heavily to the earth, turning along its long axis. A long black flag of smog follows it. A crew member tries to climb out of the upper part of the fuselage. He gets free, but his parachute is burning. Poor fellow! His somersaulting body falls after the spinning fuselage of the fatally hit Liberator. At 1,000 meters above the earth a violent explosion rips the wreck.

Burning single parts fall two, three hundred meters along the runway of Zwischenahn airport near a farm that is immediately set on fire by the gas from the plane's tanks. In its insane descent to the ground, I follow my booty and land on the runway below me. I roll my machine in the direction of the

Republic P-47 Thunderbolt fighter delivered by sea from the USA to England.

burning farm, turn my engine off, and swing out of my seat. I hurry to the crash site. There is a crowd of people there trying to put out the barnyard fire. I help move furniture, animals, and appliances out of the smoke and flames to safety. The smoke bites my eyes, takes my breath, and the flames singe my flying suit as I pull a pitifully squealing pig on its hind paws out of a burning stall. The stall burns to the ground. The house and the barn are saved. What is left of the Liberator is scattered in an animal enclosure. When the machine exploded in mid-air, the crew were blown out. With limbs broken a hundred times they lay close to one another among the smoking rubble. Hundred meters further on the other side of an earthen wall, I find the pilot's seat along with the nose wheel. Undamaged, a doll, a mascot, sits next to the splintered cockpit glass.

An hour later I land at Jever. My men carry me on their shoulders to the dormitory. That was my fourth combat victory, on my 164th operational mission. I cannot help thinking about the bodies of the American crew. When will our turn come? Those men share in common with ourselves the great adventure of flying. Separated for the moment by the barrier of war, we shall one day be reunited by death in the air."[19]

Pilots of I./JG 1 reported shooting down a total of 8 four-engine bombers during that action (Lt. Knoke, Oblt. Frey, Uffz. Demetz, Fw. Wennekers, Lt. Gerhardt, Ofw. Dobrick, Fw. Raddatz and Oblt. Sommer) without any losses. In combat with I./JG 1 Americans lost five B-17s, including two of 91. BG ("Kickapoo" flown by Capt. John Swais and "Short Snorter II" flown by 1/Lt. Beaman E. Smith) and three from 305. BG. B-17 of 305. BG, flown by George E. Stallman, was the first to be shot down. The remaining two Flying Fortress bombers lost by 305. BG were flown by Capt. Edwart E. Tibbet ("Arkie", all crew members survived) and by Lt. Isaac D. Benson ("Devil's Playmate", the entire crew perished).

Twenty minutes later, at about 11.50, American formation was attacked by the fighters of III. and IV./JG 1. Germans reported shooting down three B-24s (Uffz. Hanke, Uffz. Doppler and Lt. Marxen) and one B-17 (Hptm. Specht) without any losses.

The Luftwaffe pilots reported a total of 15 four-engine bombers shot down with a loss of a single Bf 110 and its two crew members of IV./NJG 1. Americans confirmed the loss of seven bombers (five B-17s and two B-24s) and one B-24 was damaged to such an extent that it had to be scrapped. Seventy-three airmen were killed and fourteen wounded. Air gun-

P-47C Thunderbolt fighter of 56. FG.

Formation of 56. FG Thunderbolts during a training flight over England. Maj. Horace "Pappy" Craig, flying P-47D-1-RE, s/n 42-7870, LM•R is leading the formation.

ners claimed shooting down 21 Luftwaffe aircraft and 9 were reported as probable kills.

On February 27, 1943, sixty-three B-17s and fifteen B-24s took part in a bombing raid against Brest. Sixty bombers reached the objective and between 14.56 and 15.00 dropped 155,000 kg of bombs. However, they failed to inflict any significant damage. American formation was escorted by one wing of Spitfires, which repulsed the attack of 8./JG 2. Uffz. Friedrich May and Uffz. Heinz Butweweg shot down one Spitfire each. Germans sustained no losses.

Due to intensification of American bombing raids against targets near the French coast, as well as those on the German homeland, improving combat readiness of their units, increasing the number of their aircraft, as well as the number of airfields and auxiliary airfields became a necessity for the German air force command in the West. A change of tactics for fighter units flying in defence of the Reich was also necessary. To date formations of American bombers were attacked by groups of fighter in strength of a squadron or sometimes two squadrons, that was 15 to 20 machines. To break tight 'combat box" formation a larger number of fighters, at least 50 or more, was needed.

Another operation conducted by the 8. USAAF over German took place on March 4, 1943. Seventy-one Boeings' objective was a transshipment depot at Hamm. Due to terrible weather conditions only 16 bombers reached the target, while the rest dropped their bombs on secondary objectives in the Netherlands, e.g. harbour facilities at Rotterdam. Again, pilots of JG 1 took on themselves the task of repulsing the Americans. Aircraft of 3./JG 1 and II./JG 1 were the first to attack. Uffz. Range of 3./JG 1 and Uffz. Kolschek of 4./JG 1 shot down a B-17 each. The returning bombers were intercepted on their way to England by II. and IV./JG 1. Hptm. Wickop and Fw. Hutter of 5./JG 1, Fw. Flecks of 6./JG 1, Hptm. Schnoor, Oblt. Goetze and Lt. Pancritius of 8./JG 1, as well as Ofw. Timm of 10./JG 1 added one bomber each to their list of aerial victories. Uffz. Meissner of 6./JG 1 scored an HSS over a B-17. German losses were limited to two Fw 190 A-4 (W. Nr. 5562 of 4./JG 1 and W. Nr. 0622) and one Bf 109 G-1, W. Nr. 14 086 of 3./JG 1.

Yet again, pilots of NJG 1 took part in the daytime action. As Lt. Dieter Schmidt-Barbo of 8./NJG 1 recalled: "Because the German Fighter Arm at this time was engaged mainly in operations over the Eastern Front, and had only a few units at its disposal in the west, we were at this time called in to repel these American attacks. This meant that we had to be at readiness both day and night, and our aircraft constantly had to be modified. Well, we usually were

Messerschmitt Bf 109 G-4, "White 1", flown by Hptm. Waldemar Wübke, Commander of 7./JG 54, had an inscription reading "Im Auftrage der Reichsbahn" painted on the side of the fuselage under the canopy.

Fw 190 A of III./JG 2 damaged during crash landing.

much too late to take off and intercept the Americans. However, on 4 March, it was a different story.

10.30 a.m. I am still in bed when I receive a call from Werner Rapp (who on this day is our unit's officer in charge of day fighting). 'The whole Squadron on "Sitzbereitschaft"![20] I inform Gustel Geiger of this message. He tells me, 'What nonsense! We won't catch them anyway and we'll be too late as usual!'

'Well, we'll get out of bed anyway!'

The Chief, Hptm Liitje, has not arrived yet and I phone Werner and ask him if he has arrived with him. Werner is very excited. 'Yes, yes, I've just spo-

ken to him. Aren't you out yet? The Americans will arrive shortly over the airfield. Twenty bombers! End of message!'

Well then, I'll be off. Perhaps I will see them after all. I drive off on my motorcycle, meet Hptm Liitje on my way; he is fetching the aircrews, having slept at the Station HQ. Our aircraft are prepared for the mission. The ground crew technicians have been at work already. I phone Werner once again from the Operations shed and ask him if we should proceed with getting strapped into our machines.

Rigid construction of B-17F enabled it to return to base even if it sustained the kind of damage shown in this photo.

'Yes, where are you for God's sake? How much longer will it take you to get ready; how many crews are at their aircraft?'

'Four.'

'Good, over and out!'

I am now as eager as can be! When all the crews have arrived, I phone once more. 'At last! Yes, of course, everybody get strapped in! Over and out!'

Today I will fly the Kurfürst-Siegfried[21], a Bf 110 G-4. [...] Suddenly, I hear on my left side, where the Chief is standing, the roar of his engines, but from the Operations shed no orders have come to take off yet. To be on the safe side, I switch on everything, and there from the left they sign to 'start engines'. When I switch on the engines the thought flashes through my head: 'Keep your fingers crossed and hope no gremlins are in the engines.' The Chief already taxies in front of me. I queue behind his tail. Becker is still in the hangar and I can't see other aircraft. Out on the airfield it's a bit chaotic - in front of us a plane of the 9th takes off. Behind him cross two from the 7th, then one more from the 9th, clouds of dust billowing and the feeling that at last something is going to happen! There, the Chief is accelerating. Should I take off together with him?

I hesitate a bit too long and now have my work cut out to get out of his slipstream and the cloud of dust which his plane throws up, but I manage it. I tuck in with him and we fly in the direction of 4-Berta - of the other two only one, Heinzelmann, has managed to take off, as we find out later.

We climb steadily. Over the radio we hear wild chattering but soon this is solved too and we clearly receive the orders from ground control; we have set course for 'Caesar'. The Chief sets course, and there we hear 'Leo's' calm and steady voice: 'Mailcoach [course of the enemy aircraft] 300 or 330.'

I don't listen very carefully to what he says. It is only important to the Chief anyway. Suddenly, he waggles his wings and is speeding up. Something must be going on! I look ahead, but in vain. Our speed is increasing all the time, course north-west. We can already see the Zuider Zee in the distance. Then, all of a sudden I hear over the R/T: 'From Karin 1, message understood. We can still see them.'

I ask Schonfeld: 'Karin, that is us three, isn't it?'

'Yes.'

'But I can see zero!'

'Me too.'

Then all at once I see them, in front of us and a little to the right. They are almost over us already. They are cruising along 2,000 metres higher than us, quite a lot of them, four-engined, in close formation. A flight of three on the right outer side of the box, which are not as closely tucked in as the rest, formed vapour trails, which in turn formed black streaks against the blue sky - a very powerful sight. Slowly, we get closer, and now we can see them well. They are Boeings, painted brown on top, which look like dorsal fins. One of them is trailing a bit.

Our fighters have arrived at last — one or two carry out head-on attacks and streak straight through the formation and the bombers tuck in even more closely together. Heinzelmann is still flying behind me and now we're at the same height as the formation, sixteen in all. Occasionally, the fighters press home their attacks, but they don't attack in close formation. From behind, another one or two Me 110s have arrived at the scene, and one of the 'Amys' that trailed a bit has regained his position in his box. The three of us slowly but steadily fly over the formation and overtake the bombers.

'We will go in for a head-on attack.'

'Understood. Understood.'

We are ready. Every now and then I squint at the Boeings. They are now to the right, behind and underneath us. The leading bombers are taking pot shots at us. One can see the threads of the tracer bullets. The weather is fine, a bit hazy but the sky is cloudless. A little while ago the haze in front of us looked like clouds and the 'Amys' descended to get shelter in the clouds, but it was nothing.

In the meantime we have arrived over the mouth of the Zuider Zee, just to the west of Texel, time 11.30 a.m. The Chief is curving towards the formation. I turn with him and there I already have the 'Amys' in front of my nose. We go in a bit from the right to the left. The automatic gunsight is on. Full throttle, and there we go in. I immediately have one in my sights. Aim is in front of him. Press the tit! The guns roar and dust flies around. The tracer curves away over him. Aim a little lower. Press the tit again and I race past him already. There is the next one. Aim precisely. Cracking and banging. Dirt flies around in the cockpit, into my eyes. This time the tracers disappear in his fuselage and wing roots and I flash past. I see no one in front of me any more. What next? One instant I don't know where to head to. There I see in front of me a Me 110 breaking off and curving down. I follow him. The fat one [Schonfeld] gave them a burst with his twin pop guns when we curved away; twenty-eight bullets!

'Are you still alive?'

'Yes.'

'No damage?'

'No.' With me everything is OK. Both engines still running smoothly. Can't see any hits. Great. I look over my shoulder. I'm now underneath and to the right of the formation. As we flew through the formation, I saw one of the leading bombers

B-17 aircraft of 305. BG during the air raid against Lorient on March 6, 1943.

Some of B-17F "The Dutchess" crew members, from the left: Sgt. Joe Worthington, T/Sgt. Jim Wilson, Sgt. R. Raubach, Sgt. Francis Gallant and Sgt. Sid Jackson.

peeling off and plunging towards the earth, as if to crash-land on Texel. In front of me I see a pair of Me 110s, without flame dampers as far as I can see, so they are from Leeuwarden (IV./NJG 1, led by Hptm. Jabs and Sigmund). Where the Chief is, I can't tell. A short distance off Texel, one bomber plunged into the sea. A column of black and white smoke still hangs over the ripples in the water. Another one has sheered off from the formation. I see him to the left and underneath me. Just when I decide to finish him off, I watch how an Me 110 in front of me raced up to the aircraft, and at the same time several Fw 190s also went into the attack, so there is no need for me to share in this! There is no one left near the formation. The Me 110s have also disappeared. We get in touch with the Chief. He will touch down at Bergen. His engines were damaged, but this was not caused by hits during the engagement; the driving unit of the fuel pump had crammed into the engine, so he has to have an engine change."[22]

Hptm. Jabs, Lt. Köster and Hptm. Jüthe, all of NJG 1, reported a single victory each. Most probably, the Flying Fortress bombers, which had been shot down were B-17F, 42-5370, flown by Lt. Henderson, B-17F, 41-24512, "Rose O'Day", flown by Lt. Felton and B-17F, 41-24464, "Excalibur", flown by Lt. Brill.

The NJG 1 night fighter wing lost two crews and two aircraft. Finally, the Luftwaffe pilots involved in that operation were credited with 10 confirmed aerial victories over four-engine bombers (II./JG 1 – four, III./JG 1 – two, IV./JG 1 – one and NJG 1 – three). The Americans confirmed the loss of five bombers, further 24 machines were damaged. Air gunners claimed shooting down 16 enemy fighters, 3 as probable kills and four as damaged.

On March 6, 1943, American strategic bombers conducted two operations over France. Formation of fifteen B-24s of the 44. and 93. BG escorted by approximately 60 Spitfires flew a diversion over the Brest harbour. At 14.00, twenty Fw 190 A fighters of III./JG 2 were scrambled from the Brest-Guipavas airfield to repel that raid. Additionally, eight Bf 109 G fighters of 11./JG 2 were also sent to that area. At 14.23, Americans dropped 44,500 kg of bombs over the harbour, but no serious damage was done. About fifteen Fw 190s of 8./JG 2 entered combat with Allied formation, but were unable to break through the fighter screen. In the dogfight with Spitfires of the 130 and 313 RAF squadrons, Fw. Friedrich May shot down two British fighters. Germans suffered no losses, but American air gunners claimed shooting down two Luftwaffe fighters and two more were reportedly damaged.

At about 14.40, a formation of 71 Flying Fortresses of 1. BW arrived over the U-boat base at Lorient. During the bombing raid which lasted from 14.41 until 14.45, Americans dropped 162,500 kg of

Mechanics of 5./JG 11 transporting 250 kg fragmentation bombs to be mounted under fuselages of Bf 109 G fighters.

Messerschmitt Bf 109 G-1, "Black 1", flown by Lt. Heinz Knoke of 5./JG 11. Mechanic is mounting a 250 kg bomb under its fuselage.

bombs which caused some damage. Shortly thereafter, American bombers were attacked by seven Fw 190 A fighters of 7./JG 2. Germans reported shooting down four bombers (Lt. Hugo Dahmer – two, Fw. Alfred Knies and Oblt. Ottfried Philipp one each). JG 2 suffered no losses. American sources confirm the loss of three B-17s and damage of further eight machines. Air gunners claimed shooting down 7 enemy fighters, two as probable kills and one as damaged.

On March 8, 1943, 8. USAAF conducted two more bombing raids. The objective of sixty-seven B-17 of 1. BW was the railroad junction at Rennes, while sixteen B-24s of 2. BW flew a diversion strike against the marshalling yard in Rouen. A dozen or so Spitfire squadrons participated in that operation.

Also, for the first time over the continent, American 4. FG, equipped with P-47C Thunderbolt fighters.

The Liberator formation was attacked head-on shortly after 14.00 by Fw 190 A fighters of II./JG 26. Commander of II./JG 26, Hptm. Wilhelm-Ferdinand Galland and Ofw. Willi Roth of 4./JG 26 shot down one B-24 from the leading V-formation each. The bomber crews lost their nerve and the tight formation was broken, which facilitated further Luftwaffe attacks. One Liberator fell prey to Oblt. Johannes Nauman of 6./JG 26, while Ofw. Adolf Glunz of 4./JG 26 shot down one of the escorting Spitfires. Commander of the JG 26, Maj. Josef Priller and Lt. Georg-Peter Eder of 12./JG 26 also added one Spitfire each to their list of aerial victories. Luftwaffe losses were limited to two aircraft: Bf 109 G-4, W. Nr.

14 984, its pilot Fw. Rudolf Holzmann was wounded and Bf 109 G-4, W. Nr. 14 990, its pilot was unscathed. Americans lost two B-24s over France (one of them was "Miss Dianne", flown by Capt. Clyde E. Proce of the 67. BS) and the third was wrecked during crash landing in England. Air gunners claimed shooting down 14 enemy fighters, 3 as probable kills and 3 more as damaged. Escorting fighters reported shooting down further 3 machines.

Meanwhile, Flying Fortress bombers were attacked near Rennes by the fighters of III./JG 2 and I./JG 27. First to attack, still before the bombers reached their objective, were the pilots of III./JG 2, who reported shooting down two B-17 aircraft (Lt. Hugo Dahmer of 7./JG 2 and Fw. Friedrich May of 8./JG 2) and one Spitfire (Uffz. Heinz Buteweg of 8./JG 2).

At 14.30, fifty-four Flying Fortress bombers dropped 135,000 kg of bombs on the railroad junction at Rennes, but they failed to inflict any significant damage. An hour later, on their way back, over the sea, west of Bayeux, Allied formation was attacked by nine Bf 109 G fighters of 3./JG 27. Lt. Karl von Lieres und Wilkau reported shooting down one B-17, while Uffz. Sigismund Dietz, flying Bf 109 G-4, W. Nr. 16 158, "Yellow 2", was killed in combat with a Spitfire.

American sources confirm the loss of three B-17s. Two were shot down over France and one wrecked during crash landing in England. Air gunners claimed shooting down 14 enemy fighters, one as probable kill and 5 as damaged. Escorting fighters added two confirmed and one probable kill.

In the afternoon hours of March 12, 1943, seventy-two Flying Fortress bombers with heavy fighter escort headed for the marshalling yard at Rouen-

Sotteville. Fighters of II. and III./JG 26 were unable to intercept the American formation, so the B-17s managed to drop 156,700 kg of bombs on their target and safely returned to base, without any losses. British fighter escort was attacked at about 13.00 near Fécamp by the fighters of JG 2. The Germans reported shooting down five Spitfires without any losses. Aerial victories were scored by Fw. Karl Gratz (84) of 11./JG 2, Uffz. Siegfried Lemke (1) and Josef Wurmheller (67), both of 1./JG 2, as well as Lt. Georg-Peter Eder (16) and Heinrich Paulus (1) of 12./JG 2.

In the early afternoon of March 13, 1943, eighty Flying Fortress bombers of 1. BW took off from eastern England for a bombing raid against the marshalling yard at Amiens. American had problems forming up and moreover, 20 bombers turned back to their bases. Only some of the sixty B-17s reached Amiens, the rest dropped bombs on random targets.

At 14.47, Messerchmitts Bf 109 G of Stab, 1. and 3./JG 27 took off from the Bernay airfield to intercept enemy bombers. A tragic accident occurred during take off. Lt. Karl-Heinz von Tigerström of 1./JG 27, flying Bf 109 G-4, W. Nr. 16 176, crashed into hangar and was killed on the spot. About 20 minutes after take off German fighters engaged fighters of the escort. During the first attack Germans reported shooting down three Spitfires. Obfw. Rainer Pöttgen (3) of 3./JG 27 shot down one and Hptm. Heinrich Setz (136-137), commander of I./JG 27, two enemy fighters. Germans lost one Bf 109 G-4, W. Nr. 16 159, "White 2", its pilot, Lt. Christian Erdmann of 1./JG 27 was wounded. While American bombers were dropping their bomb loads on Amiens, Messer-

Fw 190 A-4, flown by the Commander of II./JG 2, Hptm. Egon Meyer. Sixty-two aerial victory markings painted on the vertical stabilizer are visible.

Lt. Heinz Knoke at the tail section of Bf 109 G-1 Y, W.Nr. 14 049, "Black 3".

schmitts attacked the escort fighters again. At 15.31, Hptm. Heinrich Stez reported his 138th aerial victory, but a few minutes later he was shot down near Le Tréport and died in the wreckage of his Bf 109, W. Nr. 14 862.

Twenty minutes later Allied fighters of the escort engaged in combat with fighters of JG 2. Lt. Heinrich Klöpper (84) of 3./JG 2 reported shooting down a Spitfire, while 12./JG 2 lost one pilot in a dogfight. Lt. Heinz Urbancik, flying Fw 190 A-4, W. Nr. 0726, was killed south-east of Bernay.

Aircraft of II./JG 26 were last to join the fight with escorting Spitfires. Both Lt. Friedrich Wiegemann (1) of 6./JG 26 and Hptm. Wilhelm-Ferdinand Galland (33), Commander of II./JG 26 increased their score by shooting down one Spitfire each. Germans lost one pilot – Ofw. Hermann Meyer of 4./JG 26, flying Fw 190 A-4, W. Nr. 5615, "White 12". All American bombers returned to England. Eleven of them were damaged and 6 airmen were wounded. Air gunners claimed shooting down 2 enemy fighters and 2 more were reported as damaged.

On March 18, 1943, VIII. BC conducted Mission No. 45. The objective of seventy-six B-17's of the I. BW and twenty-seven B-24's of 2. BW were harbour facilities at Vegesack, mainly the Bremen Vulcan submarine shipyard.

At 14.42, Messerschmitt Bf 109 G fighters of 1./JG 1 scrambled from the Jever airfield. Lt. Heinz Knoke of 2./JG 1 recollected the action: "At an altitude of 7,500 metres we establish contact with the enemy in the Heligoland area. I lead the Flight in close formation for a frontal attack. I open fire on a Liberator from a little below. It immediately starts burning and sheers off to the right as it falls away from the formation. I come in again to attack from above the tail, and then turn for another frontal attack, firing from ahead and below the steeply diving Liberator. My aim has never been better. Suddenly there is an explosion, and the blazing crate disintegrates into a shower of wreckage above my head. For a few moments I am in danger of collision with falling engines or spinning flaming wings. That would mean certain disaster for me. Acting quickly, I slam the stick hard over into the left corner and go into a power dive. The falling fuselage of the Liberator misses me by inches as it hurtles into the depths. It falls into the sea some twelve miles south-east of Heligoland."[23]

The aircraft shot down by Lt. Knoke was B-24 "Hot Freight", flown by 1/Lt. Howard E. "Tarzan" Kleinsteuber, of 93. BG. The bomber exploded at 15.14 and Sgt. Louis A. Webb was the only survivor.

Four minutes later Oblt. Hugo Frey of 2./JG 1 reported shooting down another B-24.

It was probably B-24D "Eager Beaver" of 93. BG, which was heavily damaged and left the formation, but escorted by another B-24 "Shoot Luke" managed to return to its base at Harwick.

Then, Messerschmitts of I./JG 1 attacked the B-17's formation. Lt. Heinz Knoke continued his recollections: "I climb back to 25,000 feet for another attack at the massed enemy formation. Suddenly my heart almost stops beating.

Dieter[24] is in the middle of the Yank formation holding his aircraft steady following the same course. His first Liberator went down a few minutes ago. Now he wants to put the formation leader into the North Sea. The lad seems to have gone out of his mind. He keeps hard on the tail of a Fortress, blazing away at it. Tracers from every side converge upon his plane.

Messerschmitt Bf 109 G of 5./JG 11 at the Jever aircraft.

He must have become completely insane.

I dive down through the formation towards Dieter, firing indiscriminately at any of the Fortresses flying in the vicinity.

Then Dieter suddenly breaks away in a steep dive. Three thousand feet below, his crate begins emitting a trail of smoke. He opens his canopy, then pushes himself up awkwardly in his seat, and the next moment is thrown clear. His parachute opens. I fly past close to him. His face contorted with pain, he grips his body. Dieter is wounded.

Fifteen minutes later he is down in the sea in map reference sector U-R-9. He succeeds in getting himself clear of the parachute, his rubber dinghy inflates, and he drags himself into it. I fly down low over his head and wave to him. He does not respond. He appears to be either unconscious or in utter pain. It looks as if he has been shot through the stomach.

I immediately report by radio the position of our downed comrade and request help for him. Then I fly in and land. The mechanics look shaken at the news. I find no pleasure in my own success."[25]

By the time Lt. Dieter Gerhardt of 2./JG 1, the pilot of Bf 109 G-1/R2 Y, W. Nr. 14 150, "Black 6" was located by Kriegsmarine patrol boat he had already

B-17 Flying Fortress formation on the way to the target. The aircraft belong to 96. BG 4. BW which is indicated by letter "C" painted in the square on the vertical stabilizer.

Uffz. Hans-Georg Güthenke of 9./JG 1 in the cockpit of Fw 190 A-4, W.Nr. 5703, "Yellow 12", at the Husum airfield in March 1943.

died. Bf 109 G-1/R2, W. Nr. 14 145 was also shot down during that engagement but its pilot, Oblt. Hortari Schmude of 1./JG 1, lightly wounded in the head by shrapnel, managed to bail out.

Ninety-seven American bombers reached the target and between 15.31 and 15.35 dropped 268,000 kg of bombs. The 305. BG, under command of Col. Le-May, gave a spectacular show of precision bombing dropping 76% of bombs inside a 1 000 feet (about 330 metres) radius circle. It was the best result scored by the VIII. BG so far and the first such successful bombing raid in which Norden bombsight linked with autopilot was used. As a result of the raid, the shipyard suffered serious damage.

On their way back to England the bombers were attacked by fighters of III. and IV./JG 1 near Ameland and Vlieland islands. Oblt. Karl Becker (1) of 10./JG 1 and Fw. Keinz Küpper (14) of 12./JG 1 reported shooting one B-17 each, while Lt. Hans Pancritius (2) of 8./JG 1 added one B-24 to his list of victories. German losses amounted to one pilot and two aircraft. Lt. Ludwig Gottschling of 10./JG 1, flying Fw 190 A-4, W. Nr. 0590, "White 9", was killed by B-17's air gunners over the sea and Fw 190 A-5, W. Nr. 7231 was wrecked during crash landing, but its pilot was unscathed.

Messerschmitts Bf 109 G of 2./JG 27, stationed at the Schiphol aircraft in the Netherlands, also took part in that engagement and Uffz. Winkler reported shooting down one B-17. Night fighters of NJG 1 and 3 also attacked American bombers. Oblt. Wal-

ter Borchers (2) of III./NJG 3 reported shooting down one B-24. American air gunners shot down one Bf 110 of NJG 1. Focke-Wulf factory Industrie-Schutzschwarm (Industry Protection Flight) at Bremen was also credited with shooting down one B-17. The first aerial victory of that unit was scored by Flugkapitän Stein.

German pilots were credited with shooting down a total of eight four-engine bombers. American losses were one B-17 and one B-24 shot down in combat, while another B-24 was wrecked during crash landing. Nine B-17's and fourteen B-24's were damaged. One crewman was killed, 20 were reported MIA and 16 were wounded. Air gunners claimed shooting down 52 fighters, 20 were reported as probable kills and 23 as damaged.

On March 22, 1943, VIII. BC conducted Mission No. 46. The objective of seventy-six B-17's and twenty-six B-24's was the submarine shipyard at Wilhelmshaven. Eighty-four bombers reached the target (68 B-17's and 15 B-24's) and dropped 224,000 kg of bombs between 15.02 and 15.10. They inflicted serious damage, both to the shipyard facilities and U-boat bunkers. However, that bombing raid went down in history because of the new, unconventional armament used by the Luftwaffe fighter pilots.

Since the beginning of March 1943, two pilots of 2./JG 1, Lt. Dieter Gerhardt and Lt. Heinz Knoke, were testing a new method of destroying American four-engine bombers. German pilots noticed that Americans always flew in a tight "combat box" for-

Commander of 9./JG 26, Oblt. Kurt Ruppert on return from a combat mission. The aircraft is Fw 190 A-4, "Yellow 1".

mation, which gave them tactical superiority due to concentration of defensive fire. Lt. Gerhardt came up with an idea of dropping bombs by fighters flying over bomber formation. Bombs equipped with time fuse were supposed to explode among the bombers, destroying them and breaking the tight formation. It was to facilitate the later attack of German fighters with the use of standard gun armament.

Bombing trials conducted by Messerschmitt Bf 109 G and Junkers Ju 88 A with three-metre-long towing sleeves lasted for the first three weeks of March 1943. After many failed attempts the bombs finally began to hit their mark.

On March 22, 1943, fighters of I., III. and IV./JG 1 scrambled again to intercept the approaching American bomber formation. Among them was Messerschmitt Bf 109 G-1 carrying a 250 kg bomb, flown by Lt. Heinz Knoke. However, Fw 190 A fighters of 8./JG 1 were the first to attack the Americans. At 14.41. Uffz. Alwin Doppler (2) reported shooting down B-17 and four minutes Lt.

Hans Pancritius (3) downed B-24, "Cactus" of 506. BS. When the Fw 190 concluded their attack, machines of the 1./JG 1 arrived at the scene. Lt. Heinz Knoke recollected: "I have a 250 kg high-explosive bomb slung at top speed under my plane. But in the meantime we are ordered to take off, and I am not yet ready to go…

Sweating mechanics work feverishly under the belly of my 'Gustav'. Impatiently, I sit strapped to my seat.

- Come on, Hurry up!

In the meantime, the squadron climbs up over the sea and disappears from the view. The Amis had crossed the Northern coast of the Netherlands.

- Ready!

Easing the throttle forward, I trundle heavily to the far side of the field. With the weight of the bomb beneath my fuselage, I have got to take off into the wind. But as I turn to do so my machine suddenly tips to the left — a tyre has burst! I send up a red. flare. My ground crew over at dispersal

Flying Fortress bombers of 91. BG ready for take off at the Bassingbourn airfield. Their target – Wilhelmshaven, March 22, 1943. "Invasion II', flown by Capt. Oscar O'Neill, is in the lead, followed by "Bomboogie" and "Bad Egg".

Fw. Walter Mössner of 9./JG 26 climbing into the cockpit of his Fw 190 A-4, "Yellow 16".

immediately grasp what has happened. Twenty or thirty men pile into a small truck and race across the field towards me. They put their backs under the left wing and heave it up. With the engine still running, the tyre is changed in a matter of seconds.

- All clear!

The men quickly jump out of the way. I push the throttle forward and start to pick up speed. The kite begins to sag to port again, but after a 200-metre run I manage to haul it off the ground, missing the roof of Number 2 hangar by a hair's breadth.

I climb out over the sea at full throttle into a cloudless blue sky. High above me, at 23,000 ft, I can see the ruler-straight contrails of the Amis, as well as those of our own fighters curving in to attack. The battle is already in progress, the unaccustomed heavy load is making my crate damned sluggish. It takes me almost 25 minutes to stagger up to 29,500 ft. The Amis have already dropped their bombs on Wilhelmshaven as the fire and smoke far below clearly indicate. Now they are retreating out over Heligoland. I creep forward above the formation until I am level with the lead B-17. I have been under fire from below for some minutes now as I try to take a rough aim, dipping first the left wing and then the right to keep the formation in sight. Two, three bullet holes blossom in my left wing. I fuse the bomb, take aim one last time and press the bomb-release button on the control stick. My bomb plummets downwards. Climbing steeply, I bank so that I can watch its fall. It explodes right in the middle of a group of three Boeings. A wing is torn off one of them, and the other two dive away in alarm. Some 30 kilometres west of Heligoland, my third heavy bomber

plunges into the sea. There has been no sign of fire. The torn-off wing follows it down, fluttering like an autumn leaf.

Immediately after landing back at Jever, I was instructed to report to the Geschwaderkommodore. He had also been in the air at the time, and had witnessed the demise of the B-17.

- My word, Knoke, you ought to try that with the whole Staffel!

- That's the plan, Here Major.

- Do you think it will work?

I was cautious:

- If today wasn't just a fluke, we ought to be able to bring down a few more dicke Autos the same way.

Next, the Jafii Deutsche Bucht (Fighter-Leader German Bight), Oberst Karl Hentschel, telephoned:

- I'm delighted, my dear Knoke, magnificent show, congratulations! – he spoke jovially, in nasal tone. It seemed to me that he was so excited, that I began to worry his monocle would drop into his cocoa cup. The Bay of Jutland has its sensation.

The squadron was the calmest place; I think all this show connected with destroying a bomber is ridiculous. Firstly, that bomb could have been dropped by Müller, Meyer or Schulze. Secondly, it was not mine, but Dieter's idea and thirdly, there were eight bullet holes in my machine.

At night I was woken up by my bedside telephone. It was the duty switchboard operator:

- Herr Leutnant, I have a top-priority call for you from the Luftwaffe High Command!

- What! For me?

I state my name. A Major of the Reichsmarschall's staff is on the other end of the line.

- It was you who brought down the enemy machine today by bombing, was it not?"

- Jawohl, Herr Major.

I am asked to give full details — the type of bomb used, what kind of fuse, how had I carried out the attack, what were the results.

- Who ordered the bombing operation to be flown?

Ordered? Nobody, Herr Major, I simply went up and dropped the bomb.

There is a long silence. I realise for the first time that I had acted completely without authority. Nobody had ordered a bomb-carrying mission to be flown. I could smell trouble brewing. The Major came back on the line.

- I am putting you through to the Herr Reichsmarschall!

His words hit me like a bolt from the blue. Lying in bed, wearing only a pyjama jacket, I freeze to attention horizontally and bark out my name, rank and unit.

- I am delighted by the initiative you displayed and wish to express to you my personal appreciation.

- Most obedient thanks, Herr Reichsmarschall!

And that was that. Leutnant of the German Luftwaffe, a full-blooded Prussian, lying in bed wearing nothing but pyjamas jacket is talking to his supreme commanding officer. That's incredible! If Hermann only knew! I am not even wearing the trousers. I cannot help laughing at the thought as I turn over again."[26]

The aircraft destroyed by Lt. Knoke's bomb was B-17F, 42-29659, "Liberty Bell" of 324 BS, 91. BG, flown by Capt. Hascall C. McClellan. Its entire crew perished.

The idea of bombing the USAAF four-engine bomber formations was investigated further by the Luftwaffe test facility at Rechlin. However, the method was not used by other units. There was a shortage of suitable sights and devices that would measure the exact altitude difference between the fighter dropping the bomb and the American bomber, which was essential to set the bomb's time fuse. The wide-spread use of escort fighters introduced by the USAAF made the employment of that method completely impossible.

Meanwhile, during I./JG 1 attack, at. 15.23, Oblt. Heinz Sommer (3) reported shooting down a B-24 and two minutes later Oblt. Hugo Frey (7) of 2./JG 1 reported a victory over a B-17. The aircraft downed by Obtl. Heinz Sommer was "Maggie" of 67. BS, flown by Capt. Gideon "Bucky" Warne. Lt. Robert J. Walker, navigator in his crew, recollected the event: "We were coming home from Wilhelmshaven when the ship was badly shot up by German fighters. Shortly after several attacks on us, the ship was shot up so badly that we all had to bale out, in spite of the fact that we were out a bit over the North Sea. We all came down in the vicinity of Alte Mellum Island, but into the water. Sgt. Klug, the left waist gunner, and I were the first two picked up by a ship headed for Heligoland. Apparently, all others drowned, or died

Messerschmitt Bf 109 G fighters of 11./JG 26.

Bulletproof vests provided crews of American bombers with passive protection against shrapnels and rounds fired by German fighters.

of exposure in that frigid water before rescuers found them."[27]

Germans reported shooting down a total of five four-engine bombers without any losses. Americans confirmed the loss of one B-17s and two B-24s. Twelve B-17s and ten B-24s were damaged, 1 airman was killed, 18 were wounded and 32 reported as MIA. Air gunners claimed shooting down 28 enemy aircraft, 9 as probable kills and 9 as damaged.

The next operation of 8. USAAF took place on Sunday, March 28, 1943. Seventy-nine B-17s and twenty-four B-24s were ordered to bomb the marshalling yard at Rouen-Sotteville. Due to bad weather conditions Liberators of 2. BW were called back to base soon after take off. They were followed by nine B-17s, while the remaining seventy B-17s continued their mission. In three minutes between 12.58 and 12. 50, American formation dropped 209,000 kg of ordnance which failed to inflict any serious damage.

Enemy formation was spotted by Luftwaffe radar stations when it was still over the sea. At 11.46, forty-six Fw 190 A fighters of II. and III./JG 26 were scrambled, but it soon turned out that the Allied formation was made entirely of fighters and JaFü 2 ordered its planes to land. At 12.47, twenty-nine German fighters of II. and III./JG 26 were again in the air. They were soon joined by aircraft of Stab I.,

2., 11. and 12./JG 2. Soon after 13.00, north-west of Fécamp, I./JG 2 made contact with Spitfires of the escort. Germans reported shooting down six enemy planes without any losses. The following pilots were credited with aerial victories: Hptm. Helmut Bolz (16), Commander of I./JG2, Lt. Horst Hannig (92), Ofw. Willi Stratmann (14), Fw. Waldemar Ostinga (1) and Uffz. German Elflein (1) all of 2./JG 2, as well as Fw. Herbert Gumprecht (7) of 11./JG 2. The British confirmed the loss of four Spitfires of 610 RAF Squadron.

At the same time Messerschmitts Bf 109 G of 12./JG 2 attacked the B-17 formation. At 13.05, Commander Lt. Georg-Peter Eder (17) reported shooting down a Flying Fortress, but he was wounded and his plane, Bf 109 G-4, W. Nr. 14 988, "Blue 1", was damaged by well-aimed fire of air gunners and it was wrecked during crash landing at Beaumont-le-Roger.

Between 13.23 and 13.25, B-17 returning to their bases were attacked near the English coast, between Eastbourne and Brighton, by twenty-eight Fw 190 of II./JG 26, but without apparent success.

Germans reported shooting down a total of one B-17 and 6 Spitfires. Americans confirmed the loss of one B-17, nine others were damaged, one airman was wounded and 10 reported as MIA. Air gunners claimed shooting down 5 aircraft, 4 as probable kills and 1 as damaged.

On Wednesday, March 31, 1943, VIII. BC conducted Mission No. 48. Seventy-eight B-17s and twenty-four B-24s were ordered to bomb the Rotterdam harbour. Severe weather conditions forced four out of six BGs to return to their bases. Finally, only thirty-three bombers reached the objective and at 12.25 dropped 99,000 kg of bombs, most of which were carried off towards the city by strong winds. As a result, 326 Dutch civilians were killed.

Americans suffered heavy losses, two B-17s ("Ooold Soljer" and "Two Beauts" of 303. BG) were lost in mid-air collision, B-17 "Southern Comfort", attacked by Uffz. Peter Crump of 5./JG 24, caught fire between engines No. 1 and No. 2, but its pilot, Hugh Ashcraft managed to fly the plane back to England, where the entire crew bailed out to safety. Oblt. Stammberger (4) of 4./JG 26 added B-24D "Satan's Chariot" of 409. BS, 93. BG to his list of aerial victories. Its pilot 1./Lt Bill F. Williams and the entire crew perished. Americans confirmed the loss of three B-17s and one B-24, one B-24 and three B-17s had to be scrapped. Additionally, one B-24 and four B-17s were damaged, 16 airmen were killed, 10 wounded and 10 reported as MIA. Air gunners reported shooting down 1 enemy aircraft, one as probable kill and two as damaged.

Strengthening the Reich's defence – April 1943

With the end of first quarter of 1943 came the time to evaluate the defensive steps hitherto taken by the day fighter units against the American four-engine bomber formations. It turned out that the Luftwaffe was unable to prevent enemy bombing raids and inflict serious damage to its units. On the one hand, it was due to the lack of sufficient force and on the other hand, the inadequate tactical training and lack of clear concept of destroying four-engine bombers. American losses did not exceed 5% of the forces involved, while the critical limit set by them was 15%.

On April 10, 1943, General der Jagdflieger, Obst. Adolf Galland issued "Directives on destroying large bombing raids", which were to set priorities for fighter units fighting in defence of the Reich:

"To increase the chance of our fighters' success in defensive combat and cause the large daylight bombing raids to be repulsed before they reach their objective or at least to interfere with a successful bomb drop, the following rules concerning their destruction had to be followed:

1. Each fighter unit (squadron – flight) as a rule has to attack only one and the same bomber formation. If it makes and emergency bomb drop, attack

Nose of B-17F bomber with its defensive armament. An extra 7.62 mm machine gun was added to the standard twin 12.7 mm ones.

must be broken off and concentrated on another, closest formation in sight.

2. Each fighter unit attacks before the bomb drop only such formation which had not been attacked so far.

3. The objective of the first attack is to break the formation. It must be performed in tight formation. Head-on attack brings the best results. However, it has to be carried out in such a way, that each fighter in a swarm, flying in tight formation, opens fire at the same time.

4. Following destruction of bombers should be undertaken from all directions. The more aircraft attacking at the same time, the greater success is to be expected and the more inefficient the defensive fire is going to be.

5. During the approach to the target none of the damaged or out of the formation bombers should be still attacked.

6. On approach to the target and on the way back to base, the bombers had to be attacked until they are destroyed. However, no more than a pair of fighters should be used against a each damaged bomber.

7. In a head-on attack fire should be opened no sooner than from a distance of 800 metres, in all other kinds of attacks from a distance not exceeding 400 metres. Each instance of opening fire sooner is a waste of ammunition.

8. Target of each attack is a single plane. Any forms of distraction or other manoeuvres do not lead to success in combat with bomber formation.

9. A hit can be scored only by setting and holding on to precise targeting point, not by firing according to tracers trajectory.

10. All attacks at an angle exceeding 30 degrees are ineffective.

11. Engagement has to be continued also in the heavy anti-aircraft fire conditions, in anti-aircraft artillery zones and closed zones."[28]

Division of limited forces at the Luftwaffe's disposal inside protected regions was another problem. So far the USAAF four-engine bombers were striking at targets located in France or on the North Sea coast of Germany. On almost the entire route to the target bomber formations were protected by Allied fighter escort. The problem that faced Luftwaffe's high command was to decide the most appropriate moment to attack the bombers. For propaganda and political reasons, Herman Göring, Commander in Chief of the Luftwaffe, was of the opinion that German aircraft should attack American bomber formations as soon as possible, that was "before they are in sight of German population". That meant for German fighters to begin their attack when the bombers were still over the sea, regardless of the Allied fighter escort presence. General der Jagdflieger, Adolf Galland presented a different point of view:

Fw. Erich Führmann of 5./JG 11 standing at Bf 109 G-1, "Black 9" fighter.

On April 1, 1943 the following units constituted the daytime Reich Defence

Unit	Airfield	Aircraft type		Pilots	
		Total	Operational	Total	Combat ready
Stab/JG 1	Schiphol	Fw 190 A	2	2	2	2
I./JG 1	Deelen	Fw 190 A	34	26	?	?
II./JG 1	Woensdrecht	Fw 190 A	34	25	48	32
I./JG 3	Mönchengladbach	Bf 109 G	37	14	48	0
Stab/JG 11	Jever	Bf 109 G	0	0	0	0
I./JG 11	Husum	Fw 190 A	40	27	45	34
II./JG 11	Jever	Bf 109 G	36	26	52	29
2./JG 27	Leeuwarden	Bf 109 G	12	9	?	?
III./JG 54	Oldenburg	Bf 109 G	39	32	40	33
		Total:	234	161	245	140

"I was of the opinion that with the existing shortage of fighter aircraft only a central defence rather than an outer defence ring could promise any success. Squadrons and wings of fighter planes in the inner circle was my idea, rather than a few flights in the outer circle. With my idea one had to accept the shortcoming that the American forces penetrated far into our territory in full daylight before they could be attacked by our fighters and that, according to circumstances, distant areas and targets remained outside the range of our now-concentrated fighter force and could not be covered at all."[29]

Even if Hermann Göring had not yet comprehended the danger posed by first American bombing raids against targets on the north-western peripheries of the Reich, it had been perfectly clear for the Luftwaffe High Command that Reich Air Defence with about 120 fighters would not be able to repel another attacks of 50 or even 100 bombers. The first reaction was to redeploy single units from other fronts back to the Reich's territory. By the end of March 1943, I./JG 2, parts of I./JG 27, III./JG 54 and 4./JG 54 had been back in the West.

Since it turned out to be insufficient, a decision was taken to form a new Reich Defence wing designated JG 11. Due to the fact that training of the unit's green personnel would take too much time, it was decided that division of the existing four squadrons of JG 1 and creation of two new wings on that basis would be an optimal solution. Thus, since April 1, 1943 the following units became part of JG 1: Stab/JG 1, I./JG 1 (former IV./JG 1), II./JG 1 and newly created III./JG 1. JG 11 was composed of the newly created Stab/JG 11, I./JG 11 (former III./JG 1), II./JG 11 (former I./JG 1) and new III./JG 11.

The division of JG 1 was followed by the change of the wing's commander. Obstlt. Erich Mix was replaced by Maj. Hans Philipp. The new commander was transferred from the Russian Front, where he led I./JG 54. He had been awarded Knight's Cross of the Iron Cross with Oak Leaves and Swords. On March 17, 1943, he scored his 203th aerial victory.

Hptm. Karl-Heinz Leesmann, formerly the Commander of I./JG 52 in the Eastern Front, became the commanding officer of the newly formed III./JG 1. He was awarded the Knight's Cross in July 1941,

Messerschmitt Bf 109 G-1/R6 with two underwing MG 151/20 cannon pods, flown by Commander of II./JG 11, Hptm. Günther Beise.

after scoring his 22nd aerial victory. The squadron was equipped with latest Messerschmitt Bf 109 G-6 fighters.

The new JG 11 was composed of: Geschwaderstab, I./JG 11 (former III./JG 1), II./JG 11 (former I./JG 1) and III./JG 11. The wing's command was given to Maj. Anton Mader, born on January 7, 1913 at Castelnuovo, Dalmatia in Austria-Hungary. Following the Anschluss he joined the Luftwaffe. When the war broke out he was the commander of 3./JG 76 and then served at the headquarters of JG 2 and in I./JG 2. In June 1941 he became the commander of II./JG 77, fighting with his unit in Soviet Union and in Africa. After scoring his 40th aerial victory, on July 23, 1942, he was awarded the Knight's Cross. Maj. Walter Spies was the commander of I./JG 11 and the squadrons were commanded by following officers: 1./JG 11 – Hptm. Erwin Linkiewicz, 2./JG 11 – Hptm. Emil-Rudolf Schnoor and 3./JG 11 – Oblt. Hans Pancritius. Hptm. Günther Beise became the commander of II./JG 11, while the squadrons were led by following officers: Hptm. Hortari Schmude – 4. Staffel, Oblt. Heinz Knoke – 5. Staffel and Oblt. Hermann Hintzen – 6. Staffel. The newly formed III./JG 11 was under command of Hptm. Ernst Günther Heinze, 7. Staffel - Oblt. Hugo Frey, 8. Staffel – Oblt. Karl Goetze and 9. Staffel – Oblt. Franz Strobl. Additionally, Jasta Helgoland, equipped with Messerschmitt Bf 109 T-2, was incorporated into the wing as the independent 11. Staffel.

On April 4, 1943, VIII. BC dispatched 97 Flying Fortress bombers of 1. BW to strike at the Renault car factory at Billancourt in the south of France. The bombers were escorted by three wings of Spitfires. At 13.49, 21 Fw 190 A of III./JG 26 and 8 Bf 109 G

Armourer of 10./JG 1 cleaning the barrel of 20 mm MG 151 cannon.

of 4./JG 54 scrambled to intercept the Allied formation. Fighters of II./JG 26 took off at about 14.10, and meanwhile, also those of Stab/JG 2. They were later joined by 14 Fw 190 A and 27 Bf 109 G of I./JG 2, as well as 11. and 12./JG 2.

Between 14.14 and 14.17, eighty-five Flying Fortress bombers dropped 151,000 kg of ordnance on

Fw 190 A-5, flown by Maj. Fritz Losigkeit, Commander of I./JG 1, covered with tarpaulin at the Deelen airfield, April 1943.

the selected target, inflicting heavy damage to the Renault factory. Some of the bombs dropped by the bombers in the rear of the formation fell far away from the target and destroyed numerous housing estates, killing many innocent French civilians.

At 14.20, on their way back to England, the bombers came in contact with first Luftwaffe fighters. These were five Fw 190 A of Stab/JG 2 and some aircraft of the JG 105 training unit. First to report an aerial victory, at 14.25, north of Evreux, were the pilots of JG 105, who managed to shot down a B-17. Five minutes later, Commander of JG 2, Obstlt. Walter Oesau (104) downed a B-17. Fighters of III./JG 26 and 4./JG 54 arrived at the scene almost simultaneously with enemy Spitfires. Germans reported shooting down two B-17s and three Spitfires. Hptm. Karl Borris (25), Commander of 8./JG 26 scored one B-17, while Uffz. Robert Hager (1) of 8./JG 26 and Uffz. Walter Holl (1) shot down a Spitfire each. The remaining two aircraft were shot down by pilots of 4./JG 54.

The next day, aircraft of II./JG 1 took part in repelling the air raid of 104 USAAF bombers against the Erla repair facility at Antwerp. Ofw. Eberhard and Uffz. Stellfeld reported shooting down one Flying Fortress each.

German losses were two aircraft completely destroyed and four heavily damaged during crash landing. Uffz. Jürgen Birn of 4./JG 54 (Bf 109 G-4, W. Nr. 19 396, "White 16") was killed in combat with B-17s, while Uffz. Robert Hager of 8./JG 26 (Fw 190 A-4, W. Nr. 2391, "Black 11") was wounded. Two Fw 190 A-4 were damaged - one of Stab III./JG 26 (W. Nr. 5610) and the other of 8./JG 26 (W. Nr. 2380, "Black 12"). So were two Bf 109 G-4 of 4./JG 54, but

their pilots Uffz. Helmut Grollmus and Uffz. Schorr were unscathed.

At 14.35, pilots of II./JG 26 made contact with the American formation, which at that time was flying between Rouen and Fécamp. The Germans were chasing after the Allies until they reached the English coast in vicinity of Beachy Head. They broke off at 15.00 and reported shooting down two B-17s and five Spitfires. Commander of II./JG 26, Hptm. Wilhelm-Ferdinand Galland (35-37) shot down two B-17s and one Spitfire. Oblt. Johannes Naumann (13) of 6./JG 26, Ofw. Adolf Glunz (31) of 4./JG 26, as well as Lt. Horst Sternberg (13) and Lt. Helmut Hoppe (7), both of 5./JG 26 reported shooting down a Spitfire each. British escort fighters shot down one Fw 190 A-4 (W. Nr. 42 392, "Brown 12") of 6./JG 26 over the English Channel. Its pilot, Fw. Karl Fackler was killed. They also damaged two more Fw 190. Lt. Hans Mayer of 6./JG 26 had to crash land in vicinity of Dieppe and his Fw 190 A-4, W. Nr. 7038, "Brown 17" was damaged in 20%. Fw 190 A-4, W. Nr. 5637, "Black 8", damaged in about 25%, landed near Villacoublay.

Last to join the fight were the aircraft of I./JG 2 and 11./JG 2. At 14.43, Fw Herbert Gumprecht (8) of 11./JG 2 reported shooting down a Spitfire and at 14.51, another Spitfire was downed by Lt. Harald Gebhart (4) of 2./JG 2. The Germans also lost two aircraft. Spitfires damaged Fw 190 A-4, W. Nr. 2467, which crash landed at Théville. Its pilot, Fw. Rudolf Alf of 2./JG 2 was wounded, and the damage to the plane was estimated at 25%. B-17s air gunners shot down Fw 190 A-4, W. Nr. 5678, "Black 7", its pilot, Fw. Hans Wind of 2./JG 2 was reported as MIA.

Among the shot down American bombers was B-17 flown by Lt. Herschel B. Ellis of 422. BS. The

Pilots of Jagdstaffel Helgoland, from the left: Uffz. Ewald Herhold, who shot down one B-17 on April 17, 1943; Fw. Erich Carius and Uffz. Oscar Menz.

Commander of 2./JG 27,
Oblt. Josef Jannsen
and Lt. Karl Wünsch.

pilot and seven crew members bailed out and were taken prisoners, while the bombardier and ball turret gunner were killed on board the aircraft. Another shot down B-17 was "Available Jones" flown by Lt. Morris M. Jones of 364. BS. The third B-17 shot down on that day was flown by Lt. Harold P. Neill of 366. BS. Its two crew members were killed, the remaining ones were taken prisoner. The fourth lost B-17 was "Holy Mackeral!" flown by Lt. Ercil F. Eyster of 359. BS, 303. BG. Four crew members were killed and the remaining four were taken prisoner. "Dry Martini III" of 364 BS., 305. BG was hit by cannon shells in the canopy and both pilots were wounded. However, they soon managed to regain control over the damaged aircraft and continued flying on three engines. Despite numerous attacks of German fighters and 180 bullet holes, the Flying Fortress managed to reach the base at Chelveston.

The Luftwaffe pilots reported shooting down a total of six B-17 and seventeen Spitfire fighters. The Americans confirmed the loss of four Flying Fortress bombers and heavy damaged sustained by further 16 machines, while the RAF reported the loss of 13 Spitfires. Six American airmen were killed and 39 were reported as MIA.

German losses amounted to four aircraft destroyed and seven damaged. Three pilots were killed and two wounded. British fighter pilots reported shooting down 14 aircraft, 4 as probable kills and 16 as damaged. Air gunners claimed shooting down 47 aircraft, 13 as probable kills and 6 as damaged.

In the early afternoon of the next day, April 5, 1943, seventy-nine B-17s and twenty-five B-24s headed for Belgium to bomb the Erla VII repair facility at Morstel near Antwerp. Their cover was provided by two RAF Spitfire wings (Kenley and North Weald Wing). Eighteen Flying Fortress bombers of 306. BG led the American formation. The leader aircraft was "Dark Horse" with Lt. Col. Jim Wilson, Capt. John Regan and Commander of 1. BW, Brigadier-General Frank Armstrong as an observer. Six aircraft of 368. BS formed the advanced guard of 306. BG, behind them were six B-17s of 423. BS and below, six bombers of 367. BS. "Clay Pigeons". At 14.35, one of 306. BG bombers had to turn back to base due to engine and compressor failure. A minute later it was followed by another one. A total of 21 bombers had to return to England due to technical problems before reaching the objective.

When the head of the American formation reached the coast of Belgium in vicinity of Ostend, the German fighters appeared. 2/Lt. Rober W. Seelos recollected: "Obviously our diversion hadn't worked. The Germans were forewarned of our arrival. We were the lead group, and they were already attacking us. I would guess that we were about halfway between the coast and Antwerp when I took a direct hit in the prop dome of my No. 1 engine. It was running wild, and, with the feathering mechanism destroyed, there was no way I could do anything about it. With the old style props and the drag from the No. 1 engine, I had to use full power on the other three engines to stay with the group, which seemed to me to be in anything but a tight formation. At least three other planes were in trouble and trying to hang in there for more firepower and protection. I called the group lead ship and told them to slow down, that we were in trouble. I got no response. For some reason I kept thinking - if only our old Squadron commander, Bill Lanford, was leading the group, he would have slowed it down and tucked the cripples in like an old mother hen, and would possibly have got us all back at least as far as the Channel."[30]

First to attack were the fighters of Stab, II. and III./JG 26, supported by the aircraft of II./JG 1. Fighters of Stab and III./JG 26 were at the head of the German formation. Commander of III./JG 26, Hptm. Friedrich Geißhardt approached one of the Flying Fortress bombers head-on from the right and above, and opened fire. However, before he performed another attack his plane was hit by the air gunners fire. Hptm. Geißhardt, heavily wounded in the stomach, managed to crash land at the Gent airfield, but he died in hospital the next day. His aircraft, Fw 190 A-4, W. Nr. 7051 was damaged in 50%. Defensive fire of B-17s also damaged Fw 190 A-4, W. Nr. 0792, "Black 4", which crash landed with 30% damage.

At the same time, that is 15.12, Commander of JG 26, Maj. Josef "Pips" Priller (84), reported shooting down a B-17. This aircraft was probably "L'il Abner" flown by Lt. Clarence Fischer, which had previously been damaged by the anti-aircraft artillery fire. Its crew managed to bail out. Pilots of II./JG 1 also reported shooting down two B-17s. Uffz. Stellfeld (6) and Ofw. Eberhard (1), both of 5./JG 1 scored one bomber each. Additionally, Commander of 9./JG 26, Hptm. Kurt Ruppert (20) downed another Flying Fortress.

In the meantime, the bomber formation of only 82 aircraft reached the objective and dropped 245,000 kg of ordnance. Majority of the bombs fell on housing estates and school, where many kids were killed. American bombs destroyed more than 3,000 houses, killed 936 civilians and another 1342 were wounded. That event made the Belgian Ambassador in Washington issue a protest note to American authorities. The remaining bombs that fell on the facility inflicted serious damage – 229 workers were killed, 78 were presumed missing, one shop floor was completely destroyed, burying in the rubble approximately 60 Messerschmitt Bf 109 G fighters, which were being repaired at that time.

When the American bombers were on their way back to bases, they were attacked by fighters of II./JG 26. Commander of the squadron, Hptm. Wilhelm-Ferdinand Galland (38), reported shooting down a B-17, flown by Lt. Kelly Ross, in the first strike. The burning engine No. 2 stopped working and Lt. Ross ordered his crew to bail out. All crew members, apart from two gunners who were killed by well-aimed Fw 190 fire, survived.

At 15.38, Ofw. Adolf Glunz (32) of 4./JG 26 scored an HSS over a B-17 flown by 1/Lt. William H. Parker.

B-17F damaged by German fighters in a head-on attack photographed after its return to England.

Only three American airmen managed to bail out. Two minutes later, another Flying Fortress was downed by Oblt. Otto Stammberger (5) of 4./JG 26. It was the aforementioned "Montana Power", flown by 2/Lt. Robert W. Seelos of 368. BS. Losses of II./JG 26 were limited to one damaged Fw 190 A-5, W. Nr. 2686 (15%), which had to crash land at Buggenhout.

At 16.00, aircraft of I./JG 2 finally arrived in vicinity of American formation. However, at that time Flying Fortress bombers were already escorted by British fighters, which attacked approaching Germans. Shooting down of three Spitfires was reported by pilots of 11./JG 2. One aerial victory was scored by Oblt. Günter Behrendt (7), Fw. Josef Merkl (1) and Fw. Karl Gratz (87). The British shot down one Fw 190 A-4, W. Nr. 5679, which had to crash land north of Ostend. Its pilot, Lt. Johannes Wiethoff was wounded.

German pilots reported shooting down seven Flying Fortresses and three Spitfires. The Americans confirmed the loss of four bombers and 13 more were damaged. Three airmen were killed and 40 were reported as MIA. The British confirmed the loss of one Spitfire of 332 RAF Squadron.

The Luftwaffe lost one aircraft and four were heavily damaged. One pilot was mortally and the other one lightly wounded. Air gunners of 8. US-AAF claimed shooting down 23 enemy aircraft, 8 as probable kills and 4 as damaged. British fighter pilots reported 2 confirmed kills, 1 probable and 5 planes damaged.

In the late afternoon of April 15, 1943, the first dogfight between Fw 190 A of II./JG 1 and new American Republic P-47 C Thunderbolt fighter, used by 4., 56. and 78. FG, took place. P-47 fighters were heavy machines with take-off weight exceeding 6,500 kg, powered by 2,300 HP Pratt&Whitney radial engine and armed with eight 12.7 mm heavy machine guns. Even the fighter pilots of 4. FG, who were earlier flying British Spitfires were surprised by the look of a new fighter. Maj. James Goodson recollected: "When we gazed at the first Thunderbolt, we thought that we were looking at the Stirling bomber. After our experience with Spitfires, it seemed huge. We were terrified at the thought of flying this monster."[31]

However, it soon turned out that P-47, with its supercharger was significantly better than Fw 190 A at the altitudes over 6,000 metres and its great weight made it possible to catch any German fighter in a dive. Additionally, it had a powerful armament and considerable range.

Despite the loss of the wing tip, this B-17F of 91. BG also managed to return to Bassingbourn airfield.

Fw 190 A-4 fighters
of 6./JG 1 at the
Leeuwarden airfield.

During a patrol over the coast of France, near St. Omer, formation of 36 Thunderbolts, flying at about 9,500 metres spotted a group of 15 Fw 190 A of II./JG 1. Maj. Blakeslee of 4. FG recollected: "About five miles west of Knokke, 5000 ft. below, I noticed five vapour trails. These planes were heading west over the sea. I turned left and then I noticed three Fw 190 heading south-east. When their pilots spotted us they headed inland. I sighted the closest, diving at 15-20 degrees angle and chased after him. I trimmed my machine for diving and noticed that I am catching up on him in a flash. His only reaction was going into even steeper dive. I opened up from about 700 yards, closed to 500 still firing. I saw my bullets flying over his canopy, so I pushed the stick and churned him twice with a burst. I noticed numerous hits around the cockpit."[32]

Maj. Blakeslee reported shooting down a Fw 190, which was wrecked near Ostend. Lt. Col. Peterson and 2/Lt. Robert Book also scored one Fw 190 each.

Meanwhile, the attacked Germans managed to evade enemy fire with an elegant bunt and withdrew without any losses. Moreover, a swarm of Fw 190s of 5./JG 1, led by Ofw. Ernst Heesen, took position behind a group of about 12 to 15 Thunderbolts and managed to shot down three of them. Two of those victories were scored by Ofw. Heesen (30-31). The Americans lost three aircraft. Capt. Richard McMinn and Capt. Stanley Anderson died, while Lt. Col. Peterson bailed out and landed in the waters of the English Channel. After 45 minutes he was picked up by a British Walrus flying boat.

In the early afternoon hours of the next day, Friday, April 16, 1943, German radar stations detected two American bomber formations escorted by British Spitfires, heading for the French coast of the English Channel. The objective of 25 Liberators of 2. BW was to bomb the harbour at Brest. At 13.30, a few minutes before dropping its ordnance, the American formation was engaged by fighters of 1. and 8./JG 2. Although the Americans, ferociously attacked by the enemy, managed to drop 52,000 kg of bombs, they failed to inflict any serious damage. The air defence of the naval base was forewarned about the raid and used fog-producing devices, which made it practically impossible for the enemy to sight the target. Meanwhile, pilots of 8./JG 2 reported shooting down three B-24s, two victories were scored by Fw. Friedrich May (15-16) and one by Ofw. Josef Bigge (5). Simultaneously, pilots of I./JG 2 who engaged enemy escort fighters, reported shooting down two Spitfires. One aerial victory was scored by both Uffz. Ernst Henning (1) and Hptm. Hans-Jürgen Hepe (11).

The shot down Liberators were "Liberty Lass" flown by 1/Lt. Frank Hodges, "Ball of Fire Jnr" flown by Lt. Frank Lown and "Missouri Sue" flown by Capt. Bud Fleenor.

American 93. BG lost a total of three B-24 over France and the fourth was wrecked after returning to England. Additionally, nine bombers were heavily damaged, 3 airmen were killed and 31 reported as MIA. British 616 Squadron lost two Spitfires. Air gunners claimed shooting down 2 aircraft, 3 as probable kills and one as damaged. The RAF fighters reported one enemy aircraft as probable kill. The Germans suffered no losses.

The second group of eighty-three B-17 bombers of 1. BW continued towards Lorient. Its objective were the U-boat bunkers and the local submarine repair shipyard. Luftwaffe dispatched a part of III./JG 2 and 11 aircraft of II./SKG 10 against the Flying Fortresses. German fighters attacked the Americans at 13.54, before the B-17s reached their objective. Fw 190 A fighters of 6./SKG 10, using their altitude advantage, dropped bombs on American formation, but their explosions caused no apparent damage. After the action, commander of 6./SKG 10 reported: "Enemy formation appeared at the same altitude, about 8,000 metres from us. As we were

Maj. Adolf Dickfeld
who took command of
II./JG 11 in April 1943.

approaching it head-on at sharp angle from the left, turning right I climbed to 1,000 metres above the first approaching wing. I was radioed the altitude and speed of the formation (7,500 m and 340 km/h). I placed myself at sharp angle on the left, rear side, over the formation, to keep my position on the enemy's side. A moment later my first swarm dropped their bombs, which explode on the right side of the formation, about 100 metres above it. My second swarm dropped the bombs on the second wing. They exploded at the exactly the same spot where the ones dropped by the first swarm. The loose enemy formation, different from the tight ones used during previous raids, was worthy of notice."[33]

At 14.05, Lt. Hans-Joachim Kinzel (1) of Stab III./JG 2 reported shooting down a B-17. Moments later, fifty-nine bombers reached the Lorient harbour and dropped 147,000 kg of ordnance. The U-boats, hidden in their bunkers, did not suffer, but the shipyard was heavily damaged. Pilots of III./JG 2 ceased their attacks during the bomb drop in fear of being shot down by their own anti-aircraft artillery fire. Soon after 14.20, the Germans struck again and two minutes later, Hptm. Egon Meyer (63), commander of the unit, reported shooting down a B-17. At 14.25, another B-17 was downed by Lt. Josef Wurmheller (68) of 9./JG 2, while Oblt. Ferdinand Müller of the same squadron scored an HSS.

On their way back to England, the bombers were also attacked by pilots of 8./JG 2, who after refuelling and re-arming their planes, scrambled again from the Brest-Guipavas airfield. Far over the Channel, Lt. Hans-Joachim Schmit (2) managed to shot

down one Flying Fortress of the American rear v-formation. In the heat of the battle German pilot flew too far, ran out of fuel and was forced to bail out over the sea near Brest. Despite the immediately launched search attempts he was not located and was therefore reported missing. The lost plane was Fw 190 A-5, W. Nr. 2705, "Black 13".

During combat over Lorient, the Luftwaffe pilots reported shooting down four B-17s and one HSS, with a loss of one pilot along with his aircraft. Americans confirmed the loss of one B-17 in combat and eight others were heavily damaged. Ten airmen were killed and seven wounded. Air gunners claimed shooting down 9 fighters, 4 as probable kills and 2 as damaged.

Another 8. USAAF operation was supposed to be the largest so far. On Saturday afternoon of April 17, 1943, two formations of Flying Fortress bombers, a total of 115 aircraft of 91., 303., 305. and 306. BG, flew over the North Sea. Their objective was the Focke-Wulf factory in Bremen.

Both bomber formations flew approximately 8 km from each other. The head of the first formation crossed the German coast at 12.34, south-east of Norderney Island. The Americans continued on the same heading until they reached the vicinity of Bremen, south-west of the city. Then, they switched to north-west, leading them straight over their objective. Between 12.58 and 13.03, 106 B-17s dropped 265,000 kg of ordnance on the Focke-Wulf factory. The losses were severe, almost half of the factory buildings was destroyed and so were 10 finished Fw 190 A-5 fighters while twelve more fighters were damaged.

Focke-Wulf Fw 190 A-4 Y, W.Nr. 581 of Stab I./JG 1, flown by Lt. Ebenhard Burath. The engine cowling is painted in black and white stripes introduced in April 1943.

The Germans were not caught by surprise, as radio monitoring stations were reporting increased American radio activity since the morning hours, which usually indicated coming of a large air force operation. During their flight over the North Sea, the Flying Fortress bombers were detected by coastal radar stations. At 10.45, one of the Luftwaffe's reconnaissance planes reported sighting of the bomber formation. Upon receiving the report that the head of the formation crossed the coastline, the Command of 2. Jagddivision scrambled four fighter squadrons and a dozen night fighters of NJG 1 and NJG 3. German fighter pilots sighted the enemy at 12.45 near Wilhelmshaven, however, due to some heading changes performed by the bombers, they

were unable to attack the formation head-on. For the next few minutes, the Luftwaffe units manoeuvred, keeping safe distance from the Flying Fortresses, trying to get into position for a head-on attack. It was only near the south-western outskirts of Bremen, when they finally attacked. Their target was the leading "combat box" made of 91. and 303. BG bombers. III./JG 54 was first to attack head-on. Its commander, Maj. Reinhard Seiler recollected: "Until 6,000 metres, I was guided by the JaFü and then as the first of my squadron I spotted a Möbelwagen[34], which was acknowledged by the others with 'Aaah!' and 'Oooh!'". Long minutes had passed before, along with my unit, I managed to get in position for an attack. Then flight after flight, stretched in

Oblt. Rudolf Strohal of Stab I./JG 1 posing at his Fw 190 A-5.

Kagero's records

B-17E used for VIPs transportation. The armament was partially removed.

a line, commenced their first head-on attack again enemy formation. Altitude 7,800 metres. There was no head-on attack in tight formation, as the Möbelwagen formation unexpectedly changed course by about 60 degrees to the left. Thus, the initial position for a head-on attack was worthless. I ordered the squadron's formation to break and commanded the flights to attack individually. That first contact with the Viermots formation took place about 40 km north-west of Bremen and my squadron was the first to encounter the enemy. (…)

During the second attempt carried out along with other machines of my Stab swarm, I managed to score a decisive hit on the leading bomber of the enemy formation from the closest distance. It was forced to abandon its place in the tight formation. On completion of that first planned attack, the formation of my Stab swarm was also broken and then I had no other option but to make the second attack against the single Viermot, heading north some 400 metres below, all by myself. I attacked it from behind and with my first burst I silenced the tail gunner. Soon, large metal sheets of the tail unit, fuselage and left wing plating started flying past me. During my third attack, when I opened up with all my guns from the closest distance, seven or eight crew members bailed out from the Viermot in short intervals. Despite my attempts to ignite the enemy machine with my gunfire, I had to stop firing as I ran out of ammunition. Both left wing engines were trailing smoke and their propellers turned slower and slower. The Viermot was in a wide spi-

ral glide, systematically losing altitude and I had a feeling that I had a plane without a pilot in front of me. As I had already expanded all my ammunition, I decided to stay close to the Viermot that I had fired upon. My fighter squadron was still attacking the enemy formation, meanwhile, another fighter squadron arrived at the scene.

Strong, western wind was pushing us over Bremen. When we were at 800 metres, the anti-aircraft artillery, not paying attention to my presence, opened up with all barrels at the mortally wounded Viermot, but they missed. At that time I was flying about 100 metres from the bomber on its right side. The anti-aircraft artillery fire went silent when we reached 400 metres. We were west of Bremen and only then did I notice that there was a pilot sitting at the controls of the bomber after all. He was going to go for the belly-landing on the outskirts of the city, as he was flying right over the ground, leaping over the rooftops of the tallest buildings. Then, I noticed that it was rushing towards one of the tallest buildings and I thought that it finally would have to crash. However, unexpectedly, the plane again made a sharp left turn clear of the building and right before my eyes it went to 100 metres into a steep climb, slowly mushed over the left wing and plummeted to the ground, exploding into a ball of fire in the middle of a barrel manufacture."[35]

Another pilot who took part in that operation was the commander of 9./JG 54, Hptm. Hans-Ekkehard Bob: "On April 14, 1943, at 12.29, I took off from the Oldenburg airfield as the commander of

Kagero's records

Kagero's records

B-17F (s/n 42-30148) hydraulic system malfunction was the most probable cause of the emergency landing.

9./JG 54, following closely squadron's Stab flight and headed for American B-17F bombers, the presence of which had been reported earlier. At about 12.40, we spotted approximately 12-150 four-engine Boeing bombers at 7,000-8,000 metres, west of Wilhelmshaven. Enemy formation was flying south by south-east. We flew past the enemy left flank to take position for a head-on attack. The head-on attack tactics against Boeing B-17 bombers was formulated because each of these Flying Fortresses was armed with 13 machine guns capable of firing to the sides and to the rear. A tight formation of nine aircraft had a concentrated firepower of 117 machine guns, which could be used against attacking fighters. Thus, it was impossible to penetrate through the barrage of defensive fire. The air was filled with so much lead, that any attempts of attack were pointless. However, each Boeing B-17 could only fire two machine guns directly ahead, which in case of a squadron amounted to 'only' 18 fire hoses (machine guns). Therefore, a decision to attack head-on was taken.

When we had just outdistanced the formation enough to launch an attack, it turned left and we found ourselves on its right flank. I corrected my heading and with the entire squadron tried

a head-on attack. At that time, the enemy formation changed its heading again and once more I was in an extremely inconvenient position for an attack, and I spotted no effective hits. In the meantime the enemy formation bombed Bremen, turned south and then finally headed west homeward. I began another attack and closed head-on on the leading v-formation. I opened fire to the aircraft flying on the right of the leading v-formation from 500 metres, still firing until I closed on the enemy almost ramming him. I saw my well-aimed rounds hitting the Boeing's cockpit and engine. In the last moment before the collision I was going to fly under the Boeing's nose, but I failed and crashed into the bomber. At that moment the tail section of my Bf 109 was torn off, while the bomber lost a part of its wing. Immediately, my aircraft went into a tight spin and naturally the controls did not respond. In a blink of an eye I decided to bail out. To do so, I jettisoned the canopy, pressed the quick-release button on my harness and the rush of air snatched me out of the cockpit. Spinning around, I was free-falling from 6,000 metres, quickly losing altitude, at 5,000 metres I decided to open my parachute. Following a strong jolt, I hanged on the harness belts under the parachute's canopy.

Kagero's records

B-17F (s/n 42-3301) of 367. BS belonging to 306. BG stationed at Thurleigh, Bedforshire. It was flown by John J. Stolz. The aircraft crash landed on November 15, 1943.

I was falling at 5 m/s, so it took about 20 minutes before I reached the ground. As steering the parachute was seriously limited, I was critically looking down at obstacles, such as high-voltage lines, forests, roads or lakes. I could land on any of them. Due to strong winds and swinging of the parachute, I hit the ground so hard that I lost consciousness. The force of impact was equal to that of a jump from a 5-metre wall (with no wind). The canopy dragged me a few hundred of metres through a corn field and when I finally came round and tried to unfasten the parachute harness, the dinghy fastening at my belt prevented me from doing so. Only when I managed to pull one of the shroud lines, I successfully rolled the canopy and finally broke free of it."[36]

Despite the sustained damage, the rammed Boeing managed to return to England. Pilots of III./JG reported a total of three B-17 kills, First, at 13.04, was Maj. Reinhard Seiler (83), Squadron Commander, then, at 13.21, Uffz. Albert Rfeifer (6) of 7./JG 54 and Lt. Rudolf Lemm (22) of 8./JG 54. At 13.10, Fw. Friedrich Erlenkämper (12) of 7./JG 54 reported one HSS.

Kagero's records

B-17F (s/n 42-31022) of 407. BS belonging to 92. BG stationed at Podington, Bedforshire. The aircraft crash landed after returning from a combat mission over Solingen on November 30, 1943. It was flown by Richard W. Lyng.

The German losses were limited to one destroyed Messerschmitt Bf 109 G-4, W. Nr. 14 935, "Yellow 1", flown by Hptm. Hans-Ekkenhard Bob and four damaged Bf 109 G-4 fighters. Two machines of 7./JG 54 were damaged in 20%. These were W. Nr. 16 151, White 2, flown by Lt. Friedrich Rupp and W. Nr. 14 971, "White 5", flown by Gefr. Rudi Wohlfahrt. Two more machines were damaged in 40%. These were W. Nr. 16 136, "Black 7" of 8./JG 54, flown by Lt. Friedrich Brock and W. Nr. 16 123 of 9./JG 54, flown by Uffz. Emil Hecker.

Following the III./JG 54 attack the bombers were engaged by fighters of II./JG 11. Machines of 5./JG 11, flying in tight formation, dropped bombs on the American formation, but due to insufficient training and targeting problems no hits were scored that day. Oblt. Heinz Knoke of 5./JG 11 recollected that action: "The Americans attacked Bremen today. We scramble with bombs, which we drop over Bremen, still flying in tight formation. We score no hits! I manage to hit a Boeing with my guns in three attempts and it starts to burn. Moments later it crashes in a field south-west of Bremen".[37]

In the almost 30-minute air combat, German pilots scored two kills and three HSS. At 13.08, Hptm. Adolf Dickfeld (132), Squadron Commander, reported shooting down one B-17. Another bomber was shot down at 13.10 by Lt. Heinz Knoke (4) of 5./JG 11. HSS were scored at 13.20 by Uffz. Paul Rohe (1) of 5./JG 11, at 13.25 by Uffz Hans-Helmut Koch (2) of 6./JG 11 and at 13.30 by Uffz. Herbert Biermann (5) of 5./JG 11. Defensive fire of the American air gunners did not damage a single fighter, but three were forced to crash land after running out of fuel (Bf 109 G-1/R2, W. Nr. 14 072 – damaged in 30%, Bf 109 G-1, W. Nr. 14 033 – 15% and Bf 109 G-1, W. Nr. 14 011 – 75%). One had an engine malfunction and also had to crash land (Bf 109 G-1, W. Nr. 14 050 – damaged in 15%). All the pilots were unscathed.

At the same time, pilots of II./JG 11 also joined the engagement and scored three aerial victories: at 13.18 – Lt. Hans Pancritius (4) of 2./JG 11, at 13.20 – Hptm. Emil Schoor (5) of 2./JG 11 and at 13.25 – Maj. Walter Spies (13), Squadron Commander. The unit suffered no losses.

The chase after the enemy bombers returning to their English bases was joined by fighters of I./JG 1. At about 13.15, the squadron commenced its first attack against the Flying Fortresses, which at that time were flying over the Friesland coast, near Wittmund. On that day, Maj. Fritz Losigkeit (6), Commader of I./JG 1, shot down his first Flying Fortress: "It turned out to be tragic for the crew of the downed bomber. The B-17 mushed left, went into a spin and hit the ground in a vertical dive."[38]

Kagero's records

Damage of the forward section of the cockpit caused by a nearby explosion of an anti-aircraft round. The pilots were the only defenseless crew members. Head-on attacks of German fighters became deadly tactics used in the later period of USAAF 8th Air Force vs. Luftwaffe struggle.

At 13.30, Ofw. Hans Laun (3) of I./JG 1 scored the second aerial victory for the squadron. Air gunners shot down two attacking fighters of 3./JG 1. Fw 190 A-4, W. Nr. 0566, "Yellow 12", crashed near Bahlum and its pilot, Uffz. Hans Pelzer was killed, while Fw 190 A-5, W. Nr. 2640 had to crash land at the Wittmundhafen airfield with 40% damage.

On April 17, 1943, pilots of Jagdstaffel Helgoland took part in their first combat mission. It was an unusual unit, stationed at a small airfield on Helgoland Island. Since the runways were extremely short, the unit was equipped with Messerschmitt Bf 109 T fighters, which were originally designed for the first German aircraft carrier *Graf Zeppelin*. Messerschmitt Bf 109 T was a naval variant of the most popular German Bf 109 E fighter with an increased wingspan and some other minor modifications. By the spring of 1943, that variant's performance was noticeably inferior to that of the widely used Bf 109 G-4. The maximum speed of Bf 109 T did not exceed 570 km/h and the armament consisted of two 20 mm low rate of fire MG FF/M cannons and two 7.92 mm MG 14 machine guns.

Precisely at 13.15, Jasta Helgoland received the order to scramble and four Messerschmitts Bf 109 T-1 went into the air, climbing at 8,000 metres with maximum speed. At approximately 12.50, the returning bombers were over the North Sea. They were being circled by about 30 Luftwaffe fighters.

B-17 G was manufactured in the largest number. The photo shows B-17G (s/n 42-40025) named „Touch The Button Nell" of 535. BS belonging to 381. BG. It was flown by Lt. Henry Putek of Chicago. During the bombing raid against Nancy, France (February 6, 1944) the bomber was seriously damaged after a nearby explosion of the anti-aircraft round. A fire broke out in vicinity of the cockpit. The co-pilot, navigator and bombardier bailed out. Lt. Putek could not jump as his parachute was destroyed by the flames. He decided to fight to the end and managed to crash land the damaged aircraft.

Kagero's records

Result of a direct hit of a large calibre round on the B-17 engine nacelle. The damage a Flying Fortress could take surprised not only the Germans, but also their own crews.

One of Jasta Helgoland pilots, who took part in that engagement, was Uffz. Herhold:

"When Carius and I pierced through the thick layer of clouds, we spotted two bombers, which had apparently become separated from the wing. We attacked the relatively low-flying Boeings. Carius was flying slightly ahead of me and although we did not expect to hit them, one of the engines of the four-engine bomber flying on the left began to burn. Since the machine was in my line of fire, my rounds had to be responsible for the kill. Carius radioed our position, so the crew, that would manage to bail out,

could be rescued. Then he spoke to me 'I have to go back, as I am low on fuel and I can only reach Borkum.' So, we were that far.

The second bomber, the one that was not hit, turned left and disappeared in the fog. The right wing of the burning bomber suddenly fell off and then its entire crew of 10 bailed out. I flew over the spot where it fell to signal them that they would be taken care of. The Americans waved a flag at me. When I circled them again, I noticed that the aircraft had already sunk and only a single man was floating in a dinghy. The others disappeared,

Kagero's records

Badly mauled aileron root and wing section. Luckily, the damage was not serious.

they must have been sucked under the surface by the sinking wreck.

I flew over the crash site at least five more times, but the only thing I saw bobbing on the waves were the wheels and oxygen cylinders. I could stay longer as I was running out of fuel."[39]

Jasta Helgoland lost one aircraft, Bf 109 T-1, W. Nr. 7762, shot down by American air gunners. Its pilot, Uffz. Oskar Menz bailed out and an hour later was picked up by the Luftwaffe's rescue floatplane.

Next to attack the returning American aircraft were the fighters of 2./JG 27, which at 12.39 scrambled from the Leeuwarden airfield. Pilots of the squadron reported two kills, but only one was confirmed. At 13.29, Fw. Paul Becker (4) downed a B-17. Meanwhile, night fighters joined the fight and their pilots reported shooting down three B-17 bombers. At 13.30, Ofw. Erich Heitmann (1) of 1./NJG 3 shot down the first bomber, then Oblt. Rudolf Sigmund (13) of 10./NJG 1 and Oblt. Walter Borchers (15) of IV./NJG 1 downed two more. Another two victories were reported by the Industrie-Schutzschwarm (Industry Protection Flight), however no details concerning these kills are known to exist.

The Luftwaffe pilots reported shooting down a total of 24 Flying Fortresses, but only 20 of these were confirmed victories. Four fighters were lost in combat and another five were damaged and had to crash land. Four more were damaged after they ran out of fuel and were forced to crash land. Only one pilot was killed and another one was wounded.

The Americans estimated their losses at 16 Flying Fortress shot down (as many as 10 were of 306. BG, while 401. BS of 91. BG lost all six machines which took part in that mission) and 39 damaged. Two airmen were killed, 4 wounded and 159 were reported as MIA. Air gunners claimed shooting down 63 Luftwaffe fighters, 15 as probable kills and 17 more as damaged.

These heavy losses, which amounted to 15% of all the bombers taking part in that mission, triggered a strong response of the 8. USAAF high command, which demanded putting 20 more fighter squadrons at its disposal in order to eliminate the Reich's defence units. Moreover, a decision was taken to suspend another bombing raids against targets in the Reich's territory for four weeks.

On April 29, 1943, 112 P-47 Thunderbolt fighters of three 8. USAAF squadrons conducted "Operation Rodeo" in vicinity of Pas de Calais and the coast of the Netherlands. At 12.58, aircraft of Stab, II. and III./JG 26 scrambled to engage them. First to sight the enemy was 8./JG 26 and two aerial victories were reported. At 13.20 by Ofw. Hans Heitmann (7) and 13.24 by Ofw. Johann Erdmann (2). A few minutes later fighters of 6./JG 26 also joined the fray and at 13.32, Uffz. Wilhelm Meyer (20) reported shooting down one P-47. The Germans suffered no losses. The Americans confirmed the loss of two Thunderbolts. Capt. John McColure and Lt. Winston Garth, both of 56. FG, were taken prisoners. Two Thunderbolts were heavily damaged, but managed to return to England.

Endnotes

[1] Prien Jochen, Rodeike Peter: Einsatz in der Reichsverteidigung von 1939 bis 1945, Jagdgeschwader 1 und 11, Teil 1: 1939-1943, Eutin, s.a., p. 172

[2] Ibidem, op. cit., p. 187.

[3] Jerrie - contemptous nickmane used to describe a German by American and British soldiers (Author's note).

[4] Bandits - nickname given to enemy planes by Allied pilots (Author's note).

[5] Bowman Martin W., Boiten Theo: Raiders of the Reich, Air Battle Western Europe: 1942-1945, Shrewsbury 1996, pp. 36-37

[6] Ibidem, op. cit. p. 38

[7] Heavily damaged B-24, 41-23710, „Hellsadroppin" of the 93.BG (flown by Lt. Julian A. Harvey) reached England, but it had to be scrapped.

[8] Comer John: Combat Crew, New York 1989, after Szlagor Tomasz: Boeing B-17 Flying Fortress, Militaria XX wieku, 6 (21)/November – December 2007, p. 20.

[9] General der Jagdflieger, Br.B.Nr. 987/42 g.Kdos., Berlin 14.12.1942.

[10] Boiten Theo, Bowman Martin: Battles with the Luftwaffe, The Bomber Campaign against Germany 1942-45, London 2001, p. 18.

[11] Freeman, Roger A.: The Mighty Eighth War Diary, London 1981, pp. 9-32.

[12] Germans distinguished three kinds of aerial victories over four-engine USAAF bombers. First was the Abschuß, which meant shooting down the plane, second was Heraußschuß (HSS), that is damaging the bomber which forced it to leave the formation and the third was Vernichtung (e.V.), that is finishing of a damaged bomber (usually as a result of the HSS). Only Abschuß and HSS were recognized as aerial victories, e.V. did not count and did not raise the score of a pilot and his unit (Author's note).

[13] Murawski Marek J.: Obrona powietrzna III Rzeszy, Działania dzienne 1939-43, vol. 1, Gdańsk 1998, p. 23.

[14] Prien Jochen, Rodeike Peter: Einsatz in der Reichsverteidigung von 1939 bis 1945, Jagdgeschwader 1 und 11, Teil 1: 1939-1943, Eutin, p. 210.

[15] Murawski…: op. cit., p. 23.

[16] The only crew member that survived was Lt. Albert W. Glass, but he lost his leg.

[17] Caldwell Donald, Muller Richard: The Luftwaffe over Germany, Defence of the Reich, London 2007, p. 76.

[18] Prien…, op. cit. 231.

[19] Knocke Heinz: Die große Jagd, b.m.w., 1967, pp. 95-98. The downed B-24 was "Maisie" of the 44. BG, flown by 2/Lt. Wayne Gotke. Heinz Knocke survived the war in the rank of Hauptmann and was awarded the Knights Cross. He shot down a total of 33 Allied planes, including 19 four-engine bombers (Author's note).

[20] Sitzbereitschaft - cockpit readiness (Author's note).

[21] Kurfürst-Siegfried or KS, code letters stencilled on the side of the plane, K was the machine's individual letter, while S marked its affiliation to the 8. Staffel (Author's note).

[22] Bowman…, op. cit., pp. 53-57.

[23] Knoke…, op. cit., p. 102.

[24] Lt. Dieter Gerhardt (Author's note).

[25] Knoke…, op. cit., p. 103.

[26] Knoke…, op. cit., pp. 105-107.

[27] Bowman…, op. cit., p. 62.

[28] Lw. Füst. Ia/General der Jagdflieger, Br.B Nr 416/46 g.Kdos. vom 10.04.1943.

[29] Galland Adolf: Die Ersten und die Letzten, München 1981, p. 223.

[30] Bowman Martin W., Boiten Theo…, op. cit., p. 65.

[31] Szlagor Tomasz: Thuderbolty 8. Armii Powietrznej USAAF, marzec 1943 – luty 1944, część I, Militaria XX wieku, No. 5 (38), September-October 2010, p. 29.

[32] Ibidem, op. cit., p. 32.

[33] Prien Jochen, Stemmer Gerhard, Rodeike Peter, Bock Winfried: Die Jagdfliegerverbände der Deutschen Luftwaffe 1934 bis 1945, Teil 10/IV: Einsatz im Westen, 1. 1. bis 31.12.1943, Eutin b.r.w., p. 112.

[34] Möbelwagen or Dicke Autos – furniture lorries or big cars, these were the nicknames used for American four-engine bombers in the Luftwaffe jargon.

[35] Priller Josef: JG 26, Geschichte eines Jagdgeschwaders, Das JG 26 (Schlageter) 1937-1945, Stuttgart 1980, pp. 196-197.

[36] Bob Hans-Ekkehard: Verratener Idealismus, Erinnerungen eines Jagdfliegers, Freiburg 2003, pp. 79-80.

[37] Knoke Heinz: Die große Jagd, b.m.w. 1967, p. 111.

[38] Prien…, op. cit., p. 291.

[39] Marshall F. L.: Messerschmitt Bf 109 T, Die Jäger der 'Graf Zeppelin', Dießen b.r.w., p. 195.

Bibliography

Bob Hans-Ekkehard: Verratener Idealismus, Erinnerungen eines Jagdfliegers, Freiburg 2003,

Boiten Theo, Bowman Martin: Battles with the Luftwaffe, The Bomber Campaign against Germany 1942-45, London 2001,

Bowman Martin W., Boiten Theo: Raiders of the Reich, Air Battle Western Europe: 1942-1945, Shrewsbury 1996,

Comer John: Combat crew, New York 1989,

Freeman, Roger A.: The Mighty Eighth War Diary, London 1981,

Knoke Heinz: Die große Jagd, b.m.w., 1967,

Marshall F.L.: Messerschmitt Bf 109 T, Die Jäger der 'Graf Zeppelin', Dießen b.r.w.,

Prien Jochen, Rodeike Peter: Einsatz in der Reichsverteidigung von 1939 bis 1945, Jagdgeschwader 1 und 11, Teil 1: 1939-1943, Eutin, b.r.w.,

Prien Jochen, Stemmer Gerhard, Rodeike Peter, Bock Winfried: Die Jagdfliegerverbände der Deutschen Luftwaffe 1934 bis 1945, Teil 7: Heimatverteidigung, 1. Januar bis 31. Dezember 1942, Einsatz im Westen, 1. Januar bis 31 Dezember 1942, Eutin b.r.w.,

Prien Jochen, Stemmer Gerhard, Rodeike Peter, Bock Winfried: Die Jagdfliegerverbände der Deutschen Luftwaffe 1934 bis 1945, Teil 10/IV: Einsatz im Westen, 1. 1. bis 31.12.1943, Eutin b.r.w.,

Priller Josef: JG 26, Geschichte eines Jagdgeschwaders, Das JG 26 (Schlageter) 1937-1945, Stuttgart 1980

Szlagor Tomasz:: Boeing B-17 Flying Fortress, Militaria XX wieku, 6 (21)/November – December 2007,

Szlagor Tomasz: Thunderbolty 8. Armii Powietrznej USAAF, marzec 1943 – luty 1944, część 1, Militaria XX wieku, No. 5 (38), September-October 2010,

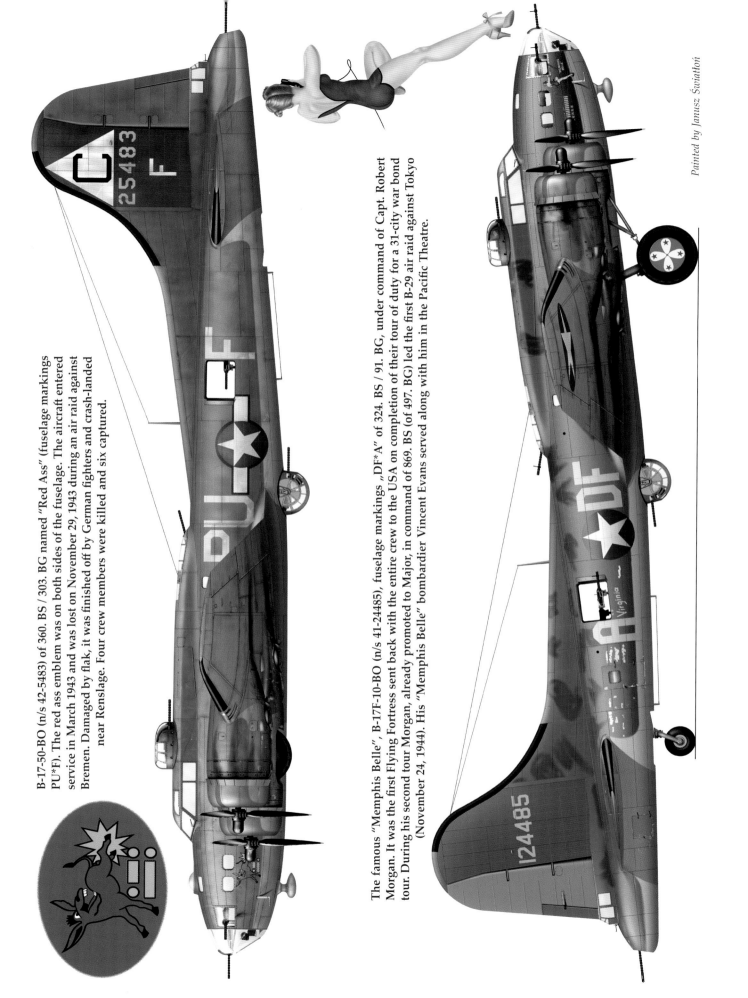

B-17-50-BO (n/s 42-5483) of 360. BS / 303. BG named "Red Ass" (fuselage markings PU*F). The red ass emblem was on both sides of the fuselage. The aircraft entered service in March 1943 and was lost on November 29, 1943 during an air raid against Bremen. Damaged by flak, it was finished off by German fighters and crash-landed near Renslage. Four crew members were killed and six captured.

The famous "Memphis Belle", B-17F-10-BO (n/s 41-24485), fuselage markings "DF*A" of 324. BS / 91. BG, under command of Capt. Robert Morgan. It was the first Flying Fortress sent back with the entire crew to the USA on completion of their tour of duty for a 31-city war bond tour. During his second tour Morgan, already promoted to Major, in command of 869. BS (of 497. BG) led the first B-29 air raid against Tokyo (November 24, 1944). His "Memphis Belle" bombardier Vincent Evans served along with him in the Pacific Theatre.

Painted by Janusz Świątłoń

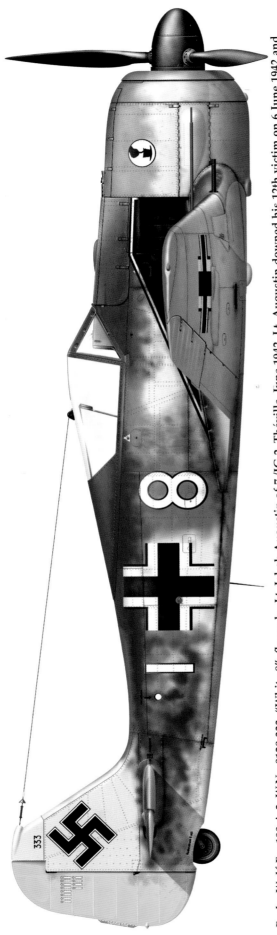

Painted by Janusz Światłoń

Focke-Wulf Fw 190 A-2; W.Nr. 0120 333, "White 8", flown by Lt. Jakob Augustin of 7./JG 2, Théville, June 1942. Lt. Augustin downed his 12th victim on 6 June 1942 and raised his score to fifteen before failing to return from combat over the English Channel in another Fw 190 A-2 on 15 July 1942. Fw 190 A-2 W.Nr. 333 was lost on 21 October 1942 when Oblt. Otto Lutter of 8./JG 2 was shot down over Douarnenez during an attack on B-17's.

Focke-Wulf Fw 190 A-2; W.Nr. 0125 304, flown by Hptm. Johannes Seifert, Kommandeur of I./JG 26, St. Omer-Arques, May 1942. Hptm. Seifert claimed his 34th victory on 17 May 1942 and then did not score another one until 1 June 1942. He perished on 25 November 1943 when his Fw 190 A-6 W.Nr. 470006 collided with a P-38 which he had shot down a moment before. His total victory account was 57, including 32 victories over Spitfires, in 439 combat missions.

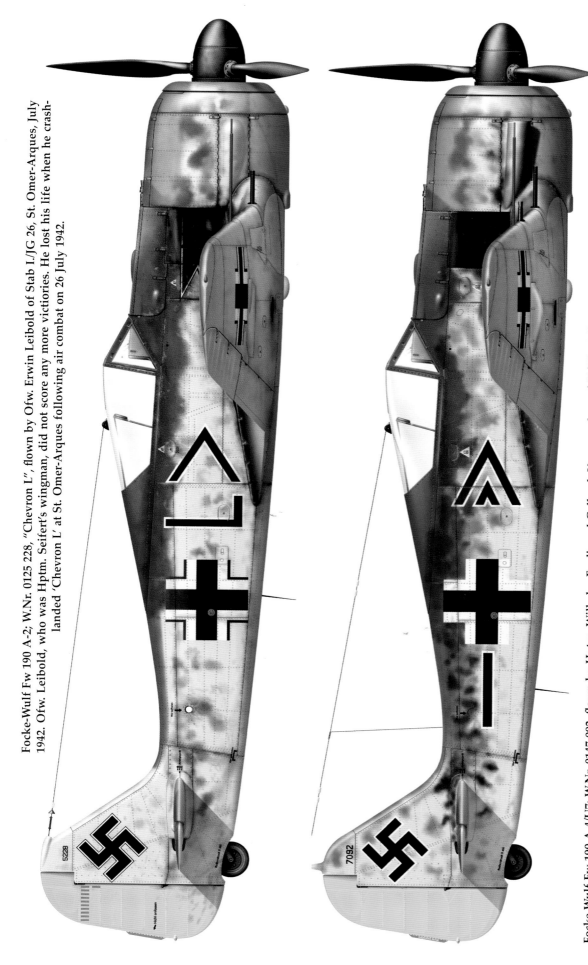

Painted by Janusz Światon

Focke-Wulf Fw 190 A-2; W.Nr. 0125 228, "Chevron L", flown by Ofw. Erwin Leibold of Stab I./JG 26, St. Omer-Arques, July 1942. Ofw. Leibold, who was Hptm. Seifert's wingman, did not score any more victiories. He lost his life when he crash-landed 'Chevron L' at St. Omer-Arques following air combat on 26 July 1942.

Focke-Wulf Fw 190 A-4/U7; W.Nr. 0147 092, flown by Hptm. Wilhelm-Ferdinand Galland, Kommandeur of II./JG 26, France, Spring 1943. Hptm. "Wutz" Galland, one of Adolf Galland's younger brothers, took command of II./JG 26 on 3 January 1943 and led the Gruppe until his death on 17 August 1943. He scored 54 victories in 186 missions over the Western Front and became one of the most successful Spitfire-killers with 37 planes of this type shot down.

WE RECOMMEND

WWW.SHOP.KAGERO.PL

AIR BATTLES 01

P-40s
of the Mediterranean

Tomasz Szlagor

AIR BATTLES 02

P-51B/C
Mustangs Over The Third Reich

Tomasz Szlagor

AIR BATTLES 03

Messerschmitt Me 262
In Defence of the Third Reich

Marek J. Murawski

AIR BATTLES 04

Messerschmitt Bf 109 T
the Luftwaffe's Naval Fighter

Marek J. Murawski

AIR BATTLES 05

P-51D/K
Mustangs Over The Third Reich

Tomasz Szlagor

AIR BATTLES 06

Luftwaffe
over Sevastopol

Marek J. Murawski

AIR BATTLES 07

Luftwaffe
over Tunisia
November 1942 – February 1943

Marek J. Murawski

AIR BATTLES 08

Hellcat
The legend of the Pacific

Andre Z. Zbiegniewski

AIR BATTLES 09

Corsairs
over Rabaul

Tomasz Szlagor

AIR BATTLES 10

Luftwaffe
over Tunisia vol. II
February – May 1943

Marek J. Murawski

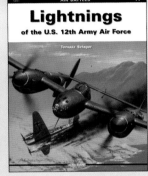

AIR BATTLES 11

Lightnings
of the U.S. 12th Army Air Force

Tomasz Szlagor

AIR BATTLES 12

Lightnings
of the U.S. 15th Army Air Force

Tomasz Szlagor

AIR BATTLES 13

**Messerschmitt
Bf 109 C/D**
in the Polish Campaign 1939

Marek J. Murawski

AIR BATTLES 14

**The Luftwaffe
over El-Alamein**

Marek J. Murawski

AIR BATTLES 15

Thunderbolts
of the U.S. 8th Army Air Force
March 1943 – February 1944

Tomasz Szlagor

AIR BATTLES 16

**Luftwaffe
over the desert**
from January till August 1942

Marek J. Murawski

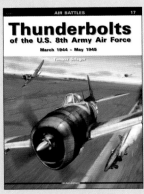

AIR BATTLES 17

Thunderbolts
of the U.S. 8th Army Air Force
March 1944 – May 1945

Tomasz Szlagor

AIR BATTLES 18

Objective: the Caucasus!
The Luftwaffe operations
in the southern sector of the Eastern Front:
May – August 1942

Marek J. Murawski